We Need to Weaken the Mixture!

GUY MARTIN

Virgin BOOKS

3 5 7 9 10 8 6 4 2

Virgin Books, an imprint of Ebury Publishing,
20 Vauxhall Bridge Road,
London SW1V 2SA

Virgin Books is part of the Penguin Random House group of
companies whose addresses can be found at
global.penguinrandomhouse.com

First published in the United Kingdom by Virgin Books in 2018

www.penguin.co.uk

A CIP catalogue record for this book is available from the
British Library

Hardback ISBN 9780753545454
Trade Paperback ISBN 9780753545478

Typeset in 11.5/18.5pt Sabon by Jouve (UK), Milton Keynes
Printed and bound in Great Britain by Clays Ltd, Elcograf S.p.A.

Penguin Random House is committed to a sustainable future for our
business, our readers and our planet. This book is made from Forest
Stewardship Council® certified paper.

CONTENTS

'WE NEED TO WEAKEN THE MIXTURE'

THE NAME OF this book came to me on an early morning drive to Silverstone, where I was going to race Jenson Button in a pair of Williams historic Formula One cars, one of which I'd helped restore. I was within three miles of the circuit, with time to spare, when I pulled into a petrol station for a cup of tea and the loo.

My mate Gary was in the van with me. When I walked towards the services toilet I looked over my shoulder and told him I needed to weaken the mixture. I knew I had to because I daren't fart.

I could tell by the look on his face he didn't know what I was talking about, and I'd be surprised if you did either. Like quite a lot of directions I've taken in life, it started with my dad. He swears by cod liver oil, and he was still working on trucks – hard, physical labour – six days a week, into his seventies, so I started taking it, hoping it would do the same for me. The difference between us, when it comes to cod liver oil at least, is he's very much a recommended dosage kind of person and I'm not.

I'll take between seven or eight of the one-a-day cod liver oil capsules every day. And I'm not talking about the little

M&M-sized capsules: no, no, no, no. The ones I take would choke a horse.

There are times, like that Thursday on the way to Silverstone, when I know I might be overdoing it and the cod liver oil is purging my system. When I have – how would a doctor put it? – very loose stools, I know I've purged the system and I need to weaken the mixture. I don't do anything drastic, I just need to knock it back a tablet, the equivalent of a quarter turn of the air mixture screw or dropping a carburettor's needle a notch, to get back on track. That's as close to a guide to life as I have now: don't do anything too drastic, just weaken the mixture.

I've started giving the same cod liver capsules to Nigel the dog, too, because he gets a bit stiff now and then. Sometimes I give him one in the morning and one at night, but if he has a runny arse I know I need to back it off for him, too.

The loose stool is the sign either of us is running too rich and we need to weaken the mixture.

We've sold a fair few of the previous books, so someone must like them. I've written this one the same way I wrote *When You Dead, You Dead* and *Worms to Catch*, writing most chapters not long after what I'm describing actually happened. That means I'm writing it without the benefit of much hindsight, but with the memories, thoughts and emotions I felt at the time still in my mind. Doing it this way means I contradict myself sometimes, like when I wrote I was never going back to the Isle of Man TT and only an idiot would do something like that. It turns out I was that idiot. The pros of writing books like I choose to, almost like a diary of the interesting, and sometimes not so interesting, stuff I do, is you're getting it straight from the horse's mouth, as it happened, with no filter.

The problem with that, at least from where I'm sat, is you're sometimes reading about me at my worst, when I'm annoyed, tired, mithered and ready to get back to the truck yard. You'll spot those bits when you get to them. This book was written over a period of 18 months and after finishing it and reading it through from start to finish, I've been a bit harsh about some people and sounded like a massive wanker at other times. I did think about changing it so I didn't look so bad, but that wouldn't have been the true story, so I've kept it just how I felt in the heat of the moment, not the more mellow view I had after time has healed the situation. I hope you enjoy it.

CHAPTER 1

'The Marrowbone and Cleaver'

THERE WASN'T MUCH time between finding out Kirmington's pub was closing and me thinking I should buy it. I look back now and realise I bought the Marrowbone and Cleaver for the wrong reason. Becoming a pub owner was purely an emotional decision not a business one. As far as

I was concerned Kirmo, the village I grew up in and still think of as the centre of the universe, had always had a pub and it needs one.

Once the thought had lodged in my brain things happened quickly.

At first I didn't think anyone was going to take it over, then I was told that someone was going to buy it. That turned out to be rubbish. Then someone else was going to buy it and turn it into a house and that didn't happen, but I was worried someone would so I rung the pub chain that owned it, Enterprise Inns, and put a bid in. They had another couple of people in the running, or so they told me. A few days later they accepted my bid. Now what? I thought. From it closing to me handing over the money was no more than a month.

For what it is, a pub, with parking, a bit of land and outbuildings, it wasn't expensive, it might have been a bit over £140,000. I'm not Richard Branson or a property tycoon, and I'm not flash or owt, but I've got a few quid, so I thought, let's keep it going as a pub. So many pubs are being converted into houses, and I understand why, but it wasn't right for Kirmo. I'm not sure if this one had planning permission for a change of use, but how long would it have to stand as a boarded-up eyesore before the council changed their minds about that?

I didn't need to get a loan or mortgage. That meant I didn't have to 'waste' money on a property survey. The

Marrowbone was a bit of a shit tip by the time it had closed, I could see that. It was tired around the edges especially the kitchen, which was a bomb-site and wouldn't pass any kind of inspection. It was what I'd describe as grufty: sticky around the door handles, and a bit of hair in the congealed fat in the corners. Even though it was years after the fag ban, there was still a stale smell of cigarette smoke about the place. Food is such a big part of most pubs' livelihoods now that it was a priority. So we needed to do it up. A bloke from Kirmington, Phil Tate, who my dad knew and lived opposite my sister, was chosen to manage the refurbishment of the place. He'd lived in Kirmington for years and he ended up doing a great job.

Phil explained the options. 'We can do it up or we can do it up or we can do it up.' I said I wanted it doing up, but not a hundred grand do it up.

Even though I always wanted to keep it operating as a pub I didn't want to have anything to do with the day-to-day running; that was the furthest thing from my mind. The Marrowbone had had the same landlord for 20 years, Robin and his wife, Ros, right from me being a lad. He was a good bloke, and would serve us underage on a special occasion. He got bollocked for it by my mum when I went home pissed on New Year's Day and puked up over my younger brother. If you had a picture of a country pub landlord, that was Robin.

After he retired it went through a few managers and landlords in a hurry, none staying for more than two years and some a lot less than that. I had a word with the couple who had been running it when it closed, and they were nice, but they weren't the right people to take on the new business. Then I had a word with my older sister, Sal, when we were out in Bonneville for the Triumph land speed job. She had previous experience in the bar world. She was the manager of Grimsby's Chicago Rock Café, where I'd also worked as a glass collector for a while to raise money to go road racing in my early twenties.

When I asked her if she'd be interested in running it I told her there was no pressure, I was just giving her the option. She'd been accepted on, and was just about to start, a nursing course, following in our mum's footsteps. I knew she was interested in running the pub, though. She couldn't stop thinking about it.

When the pub fitters got stuck in it turned out there was a leak here and a leak there and the place needed more than I had expected. It wanted a new bar because it was rotten, and the upstairs was a mess, so that needed to be gutted. We still haven't done anything with the upstairs yet. Perhaps I should have had that survey ... The pub closed its doors in August 2016 – some thought forever – and reopened on 3 December the same year. During that time I hardly had anything to do with it. Sal was sorting it, with a lot of help from Andy Spellman, the bloke who looks after the business side of the Guy Martin Proper stuff.

Sal soon decided she did want to run it, so we came to an agreement that for six months or a year, depending on how it went, she could get the place up and on its feet without any rent. After that she'd pay rent to me. When people ask me about the pub I tell them it's not mine, it's my sister's, because I don't want to sound like a flash Harry. If I wanted to be more accurate I'd explain it's my pub, but her business. I have nothing to do with the day-to-day decision-making. It's all up to her.

It's gone from closing down, owing money to the VAT man and suppliers, to a right successful place, and that's down to her. She's a grafter, like my dad, my mum, all of us Martins. Some people don't understand why I want to work so hard, getting up at stupid o'clock to work on the trucks in the middle of winter, but it's been bred into us and we can't shake it. The pub has taken over Sal's life, but she's doing bloody well. She's grafting her hole off.

When it came to decorating the place I wanted it to look different. I wondered if we could have a farm trough in the men's toilet, and we ended up with three metal buckets to pee into. I came up with the idea to have stained glass in the front door, and the design is the official emblem of the 166 Bomber Squadron, which was based at Kirmington air base, now Humberside airport, during the war. The bloke who made it did such a great job of it, with the bulldog in the middle and the word Tenacity, underneath, that if some-one told you it had been there since 1943 you'd believe them.

There's a little bit of motorbike stuff in the pub, some of it mine, some of it belonging to my dad. We put some ornaments and old bits and pieces of my bikes in there, bits of wrecked engines that I've blown up, but a lot of it was stolen by people visiting, so my dad went around bolting everything down.

There's usually a bike parked near the kitchen door. The Martek, the Racefit Harley I bought from Spellman and the Yamaha TY80 that Sal and I shared as our first bike have all been in there for a bit. There's a lot of bomber and Lancaster stuff, because it's important to the local area. There's a big antique map of Lincolnshire on the chimney breast, with Kirmo as the centre of the universe; a photo from the start of the 1950s race at the Nürburgring; instrument gauges from old aircraft; RAF patches and photos from the war. You can buy Kirmo T-shirts and our woolly hats. Ryan Quickfall, the illustrator from Newcastle who did the pictures in this book and has designed a load of T-shirts and calendars for us, designed the pub sign. It's Nigel the dog with a massive bone in his mouth, being chased up the High Street, past the church, by a butcher swinging a cleaver, while a Lancaster flies overhead.

The local brewery, Batemans, from Wainfleet All Saints, near Skegness, contacted us to say they could supply a special Skull and Spanners ale for the pub. We all liked the idea and sell a lot of nine-gallon barrels of it. Sal says it's the second most popular drink after Carling. We've kept it exclusive to the Marrowbone and the brewery's own visitor centre. The pub's a free house, meaning Sal can buy her drinks from wherever she likes, she isn't tied to one supplier, but Sal likes dealing with Batemans. And we sell Mr Porky pork scratchings, of course.

We've had a few bands playing. The opening night was a dead good covers band called Electric 80s, who I knew about because I met one of the members of the band, Terry, through filming *Speed* programmes. He works for Air Products, who supplied the helium for the balloon I was hung under for the failed human-powered Channel crossing flight.

The opening night was heaving, full of locals relieved that their pub had reopened and wasn't going to be turned into something else. Sal was brilliant, proving right away to be the best choice for the job. I hoped it would continue like that and it hasn't slowed down much since. That's down to the good grub and friendly service.

Then Spellman's band, The Lilyhammers, said they'd play the first New Year's Eve if I agreed to get on stage with them and sing. It was the most frightening thing I've ever done, because I can't sing and there was going to be a room full of people. On the way there Shazza (Sharon, my missus) had the song on the van stereo and was helping me learn it, Karaoke-style, to the original. Before it was my time, I was out of my comfort zone, sat shaking in the front of my van trying to memorise the words to 'Place Your

Hands' by Reef that Spellman had printed out for me. I was like a rabbit in the headlights, but if I was doing it, I was doing it, so I was fully committed and trying to belt it out. Then I tried 'Hard to Handle', the Otis Redding song that's been covered by dozens of folk. I suppose I was attempting The Black Crowes' version, but I made a dog's dinner of it. I think the crowd could appreciate my commitment to the cause, even if it wasn't the best singing they'd ever heard. It's good to get right out of your comfort zone, though, and whenever I hear those songs I still laugh

We also had the Ken Fox Wall of Death pitch up. We wanted to set it up in the car park, but, when he turned up, Ken realised it wouldn't fit. So, at the last minute, we set up on the playing fields opposite the pub. It was to coincide with the 166 Reunion weekend, when the surviving members of the bomber squadron turn up to the local church for a remembrance service. The pub raised £1,500 for the church that weekend, and I did two shows a night on the wall with Ken and his hell riders. What a life. I was riding one of the Hondas I'd learned on and the viewing platform was packed. There was a hell of an atmosphere, and even though I'd done it a good few times, there'd been a good few months since I'd ridden the Wall of Death and it takes some concentration and technique. Don't clip the wire, don't catch anyone's eye in the crowd. Ken didn't have to give me any reminders, or prompts from the middle; he let me get on with it.

Sal says the locals are the lifeblood of the place. She reckons it closing for four months made those who agree with me, that Kirmo should have a pub, really appreciate the place. There are some in the village who complain about the noise of the odd band we have or the racket from the Wall of Death, that was in the village for all of three days. Sal has had to deal with the council, and had inspections when bands have played and they've not upheld the complaints. It doesn't matter that the pub has been saved or that we live next to a commercial airport – people still want to complain.

My mum and dad go in all the time. My dad loves it. He retired on 1 March 2018, after 55 years, and I reckon that one of the reasons he retired is so he can put his attention into the pub. He's the handyman and groundskeeper. That one reason, that I didn't consider when I made the decision at the time, has become enough of a justification for me deciding to buy the pub. My dad has my problem, or I've inherited his, that he's addicted to work. In the extreme. Now he can concentrate on the pub. He's not getting paid, but it's enough to keep him dead busy sorting stuff out for my sister, polishing the pipes, organising the cellar, doing this, doing that, and he loves it. Sal tries to pay him, she's fair like that, but he won't have it. He's dead proud of what she's done there.

Another good thing about the pub staying open is that it's employing local lads and lasses, 21 staff from Kirmington or surrounding villages.

And that's all without me giving it much of a leg-up. I don't believe people turn up thinking I'm going to be sat at the end of the bar doing a crossword or summat, with a pint in front of me, but having my name attached to it is enough to make some people drive out and visit. It's the good job that Sal's done that keeps people coming back or telling their friends to visit. Sal would never tell me if she thought she made the wrong decision and should have gone into nursing, but I think she's happy.

The decision to buy the place might not have been the best thought out I've ever had, but it's all worked out for the best so far.

CHAPTER 2

'That ride changed me'

WHEN THE PUB opened, I wasn't long back from the Tour Divide, the ride that became a big part of *Worms*. For those who don't know, the Tour Divide is the world's toughest mountain bike race. The route follows the Continental Divide, down the Rocky Mountains. The definition of the Continental Divide is the geographical line that splits North and South America. To the west of the line the water flows to the Pacific, to the east it flows to the Atlantic.

The mountain bike route starts in Banff, Canada, and ends at the Mexico border. It is never more than 50 miles from the Continental Divide and crosses it 26 times. You can ride the route as a tourist, and plenty of folk do, but if you're competing in the race you have to do it with no outside assistance, and you're not supposed to talk to anyone you know during the race.

Other than people in petrol stations and cafés I only really met a handful of folk on the whole ride. One was a journalist who'd been tracking my ride and came out to interview me and take photos, another was a cyclist going east to west, some others were Tour Divide riders going in the opposite direction, and one was the winner of the 2016 Tour Divide, the Brit Mike Hall.

I rode with Mike for half or three-quarters of a day. It was at a point where I'd ridden up a track and I couldn't work out on the GPS where I was and I was going round in circles a bit. I had set off at three in the morning, and I could hear water to the left of me, but it wasn't showing on the GPS. I'd read my notes the night before, when I'd finished riding at midnight or whatever, but they were a bit woolly. Because I hadn't spent a bit more on paying for the more detailed GPS route (that would have shown the background) I was having a bit of bother. My Garmin screen just showed a blue line to follow. I thought I'd buy this cheaper programme and save a few quid. Having the background showing wouldn't have saved me loads of time, but it would've made it easier on that morning.

I'd just got onto the right route when Mike Hall caught up with me. I'd set off before the official start of the race because I didn't want to leave in a crowd. That meant my time was being logged by the organisers, but it wouldn't count for a place in the final race standings. If I'd have been in the race I'd have finished third, I think, so I wasn't hanging about. But if you looked at my time trace from meeting Mike Hall to the end, I was faster after seeing him, because he showed me how he was riding. I was riding with him up hills and he was huffing and puffing, and I was keeping with him quite comfortably, even though he was on a lighter bike. He said, 'You're fit, you are.' I said I do a bit of cycling, and told him I was surprised by how hard he'd push himself up hills, putting his body in what trainers and athletes call the red zone. He said, 'Yeah, I push hard, then do it all again.' I'd never let myself get to that point because I thought that's when I'd be in an anaerobic state. I'd be robbing glycogen and I'd bonk out, having nothing left in the tank. Now I was watching Mike and thinking, Bloody hell, he's bouncing the valves every day!

From that point on I thought, Bugger it. I surprised myself. I saw that I could push myself harder and still make power for up to 20 hours a day.

It's easy to say all I've got to do to beat Mike Hall's Tour Divide time is to sleep less and ride more, very easy to say. He is a special sort of boy he is, or was . . .

We emailed each other after that. He complimented me on the fact that I wasn't mucking about, I was serious about riding, and told me of some races he had coming up. He was going to do the Arizona Trail Race in April 2017; this was another race in America like the Tour Divide, but a lot shorter, only 750 miles. Then he changed his mind, saying he was going to do a new event, called the Indian Pacific Wheel Race, instead.

That year, 2017, was the first running of this big, unsupported, backpacking bicycle race. Like the Tour Divide, the competitors were expected to carry everything they needed themselves, or buy it on the road. There were no back-up trucks or teams. Mike carried next to nothing on a race like this anyway. It started in Perth, on the Indian Ocean on the west coast of Australia, then went more or less along the southern coast, detouring into the mountains before finishing on the Pacific Ocean in Sydney.

The route was 5,500 kilometres, just short of 3,500 miles, and made a point of calling in at cities along the route, which was a big difference to the Tour Divide. The American race route visited the odd small town, but mainly villages of a few houses and a diner or petrol station at the most, and only so riders could get food and drink.

Mike was in second place in the race, coming out of Australia's capital, Canberra, less than 250 miles from the end, when he was hit by a car at half six in the morning, on 31 March 2017, and died at the scene.

Mike will stick in my mind. I think anyone who does well in these kinds of events and keeps going back for more has issues, demons in their head, something that makes us keep wanting to punish ourselves. I still want to but it's out of step with where I've found myself in life, with Shazza, Dot, the nice house and no shortage of opportunities . . . I've worked hard for what I've got. Do I feel guilty, subconsciously? Is that why I get up at four o'clock to cycle through freezing rain to work on trucks?

I was thinking about all this the other day, and realised that if I had to pick one of the moments when I was the happiest, or most content, in my life it was on the Tour Divide.

I'd left Salida on a tough climb, up and over Marshall Pass. It wasn't the steepest climb on the route, just an uphill drag for a good five hours at the pace I was pedalling. It just kept going until it reached the summit at nearly 11,000 feet (two and a half times the height of Ben Nevis, Britain's tallest mountain). After that I'd come down the other side to a filling station with a café, in a little village called Sargents in Colorado. There had been snow at the top of the pass, but it was hot at the bottom. The café was just closing up as I arrived, at about eight or nine at night, but the woman was kind enough to stay open for me to buy some grub and Gatorade. While I was there a couple of push-bikes, all kitted out for solo racing, arrived. You can do the Tour Divide from north to south, like I'd chosen, or south to north. These lads were going northbound.

I'd left Banff a couple of days before the official start, and I hadn't been hanging about, so other than the few hours I'd spent cycling with Mike Hall this was the first time I'd met anyone in the race. I told them I was Terry from England. I'd entered under a false name, because I thought some magazines might have sent folk out to try to photograph or interview me on the route and I wanted to keep myself to myself. None of the people who'd served me sandwiches in Subways or pizzas in tiny towns knew, or cared, who I was, but here was a chance for me to get into character. One of riders was from Chicago, but had spent a lot of time in England teaching at a university. He was explaining that his rear hub had exploded on his bike, so he needed to get a lift to somewhere to get a replacement. There was another lad, an old boy, but I got the impression he was fast. I don't know why, but I've never felt as at home as I did when I was talking with them. Then the lassie who ran the café said she could make us some extra sarnies, and they were good, wrapped in tinfoil. There were so many calories in them you needed a forklift to pick them up. The northbound lads were camping there overnight, but I had another three hours' riding in me before I bedded down.

I didn't talk for long, but I'd enjoyed having a yarn with someone on the same wavelength and with the similar plan in mind. The moment when I biked down the road, away from the café in Sargents, the sun just going down, is one of the moments I look back on as the happiest I've ever been. What does that say?

A few days later the ride was over. The last stretch, through the bottom of New Mexico, was a 60-mile straight road with a border station at the end. I didn't know what was going to happen, or if Sharon was going to be there. I crossed the finish line and I hadn't spoken to anyone I knew for over three weeks. When I got to the end I started crying. What am I doing? I'm a hard man, but what I'd put my brain and body through during those 18 days and 7 hours, and in the build-up to crossing the finish line, set me off. I had to have a word with myself. Nothing has ever made me cry like that. There isn't a motorcycle race in the world that would make me cry like that.

Even though I wrote about the Tour Divide in *Worms to Catch,* it's made such a big impact on how I think about things since that I've mentioned it a lot in this book. On the Tour Divide you can be climbing for days. In times like that you could sit and cry or shout and swear till you lost your voice, and it doesn't make a shit's worth of difference, you've just got to get on with it. That's what I learned. Channel your energy into reaching the finish line. That ride changed me, it changed my life.

CHAPTER 3

'The TV lot knew something wasn't right'

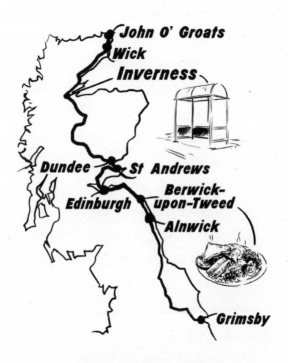

THE TOUR DIVIDE was something else, and if I could get that feeling again, from another experience, I wanted to. After I got back in June 2016, it didn't take long to come up with an idea of riding to Magadan, a port town on the Sea of Okhotsk in the far east of Russia, but I don't know when I'm going to do it. Especially not now since Dot arrived in October 2017 (but more about her later). It'll take six weeks, if everything goes smoothly – 200 miles a day for six weeks, with loads of river crossings, where I could be stuck for ages waiting for a truck to hitch a lift over the water if I couldn't cross it without being swept away. Part of me thinks I've got so much to learn before attempting it, while the other part thinks, Bugger it, I'll just set off and cross the bridges, or rivers, as I come to them.

So, with Magadan too much to take on with everything else that was happening at the time, the TV lot came up with a load of rare pushbike challenges, and one of them was riding around the coast of Britain. I looked at the record, set in 1984 by Nick Sanders, who is better known as a motorcycle distance record holder. He set it at 22 days and I looked at it, did a few quick sums in my head and told the TV bods I reckoned I could ride around the coast of Britain in 20 days. I added that I'd set off the first week in December, so I'd finish the ride on Christmas Day. That side of things was my idea.

As part of the filming I met up with Nick Sanders. He's definitely a doer. He's made a job out of breaking long-distance records, mainly on motorbikes, but he was a professional cyclist years ago, I think. He has a very weathered appearance. The time he set was very impressive.

I came back from the Tour Divide and worked like hell on the trucks, then went to China to film the *Our Guy in*

China programmes. As part of that I did a ride through the Taklamakan Desert. It wasn't far, 347 miles, non-stop. I did 300 miles in 24 hours, only stopping to eat and run behind a sand dune for a leak every now and then. I'd done enough 24-hour Strathpuffer bike races that I know what it's like to cycle for 24 hours and how much effort I can put in at the beginning and still be going at the end. Plus, because this was not far off the back of the Tour Divide, it didn't feel like much of a challenge. I had all the TV crew and all the health and safety folks that TV demands. They didn't need to do anything, but insurance policies and risk assessment forms say they've got to be there just in case, so that's the way it is. I didn't need them for the Tour Divide, but I know the TV lot have to dot the i's and cross the t's. I did get a monk on when they were driving right in front of me filming and chucking up sand and blowing diesel fumes in my face. The previous record for this desert crossing was 47 hours and I did it in 28 hours and 17 minutes, an average of near enough 12mph.

When I got back from China I was back at Mick Moody's truck yard in Grimsby, playing catch-up, doing a few jobs on Scanias he'd taken in on part-exchange and getting stuff ready for MOTs, and doing other bits because it wasn't long before I had to fly out to New Zealand for a week at the Burt Munro Challenge in his home town of Invercargill.

Burt Munro is the man whose story of record-breaking at Bonneville Salt Flats, in Utah, on his home-built special, was made into the 2005 film *The World's Fastest Indian*. The Burt Munro Challenge was a week of motorbike races, of all types, to celebrate this legend, who died in 1978.

I was only interested if I could take part on my own bike, so my Martek was shipped out. It's the turbo Suzuki special that I've owned for years and raced at the 2014 Pikes Peak International Hill Climb in Colorado. Me and Shazza followed it out to New Zealand, and had a great time. I'd been a few times before, for the Wanganui Road Races that take place on Boxing Day on the Cemetery Circuit, and I love the country. The people are great and it's so laid back. It's a bit backward, there's loads of open space, no one seems to be in a rush.

We had a couple of days without bikes. One day I went out with a group for a 40- or 50-mile mountain bike ride and Sharon arranged to meet up on the ride and for us to do a bungee jump together, at the 43-metre AJ Hackett Kawarau Bridge Bungy, the world's first permanent bungee site. Neither of us had done one before and I thought she might select reverse when she saw it but she didn't and it was mega to do it together.

The rest of the time I was in a shed working on the Martek. It was nothing but trouble, but I liked mucking about with it. I did a couple of track days, at Teretonga racetrack, a ten-minute drive from Invercargill. I borrowed a van, paid $40 and I had the track nearly to myself. What a life. I'd be having all this grief with the bike, not sure why it wasn't running right, then I'd find myself on track with a new Fireblade or a BMW S1000R and I'd smoke them on this thing concocted in my shed, and it was the best feeling in the world. Then something would go wrong again, but it was all worth it for those moments.

When I was in New Zealand I caught a right stonking cold, the last thing I needed, on top of a 28-hour journey home, before starting something like the ride I had planned. I was back for three or four days, working at Moody's, before the start of the round Britain ride. Oh, and the pub I'd bought was opening the night before I set off. Like I said, busy.

John, from Louth Cycles, built me another bike, a new version of what I'd done the Tour Divide on. This time it was a Salsa Cutthroat, not the Salsa Fargo I'd ridden through North America on. Salsa is a California-based company and they describe the Cutthroat as a 'Tour Divide-inspired, dropbar mountain bike'. It sounded perfect and looked trick, kitted out with Hope parts, all made in England. It was a step up from the Fargo.

I was bunged up with snot and cold, and the last thing I should've been doing was getting on a pushbike before the big ride, but I hadn't ridden this new bike at all so I set off to work and back, on a cold December morning, just to make sure everything was all right. It was, so I didn't sit on a pushbike again until I set off three days later. I just worked on the trucks, blew my nose and slept.

The idea was to start in Grimsby, and ride the whole circumference of Britain in 20 days. When I'd helped come up with the idea I thought I could piss it.

The TV lot had got Garmin involved and they'd made a full route plan, coming up with one of 4,866.6 miles. The current record was 4,838 miles, set in 1984. New one-way roads along stretches of coast must have made the difference. Garmin also worked out there was 69,443 metres of climbing, the equivalent of riding the height of Everest nearly eight times in 20 days. Everyone had put loads of effort in, to make sure it all went smoothly. The only fly in the ointment was me.

Even though the Garmin route was clockwise, heading south from the Grimsby start point, I'd decided I would head north, because there was a good chance I'd get a tail wind up the north-east coast of England and the east coast of Scotland.

The pub opening was great, and I slept in Kirmo at my sister's, Sal, on the Saturday and got up at three in the morning to get to the start in Grimsby. I wanted to be in Scarborough for nine that morning.

Two of my mates, Dobby, whose house I rented in Caistor when I moved out of Kirmington, and John, a potato merchant and a keen cyclist, rode with me on the first day. The route was all on road. I was doing a bit of work, but for most of it I was in the slipstream of those two boys, taking it a bit easy.

The weather was cold but mint on that first day. I was probably 100 miles into the ride and thought, Something isn't right here. But I kept quiet. I just thought I had to man up.

Dobby and John ran out of steam after about 150 miles, near Newcastle, got picked up and given a lift home. I got to Alnwick, and I was on schedule. Shazza was following in the Transit, doing the support truck side of things. So I kipped in the van. Everything was still on schedule at the end of the first day, but my Achilles was giving me bother.

I slept for four or five hours, woke up at four in the morning, got on my bike and, after struggling to find anywhere else to eat, headed to Berwick-upon-Tweed for breakfast. I had a massive fry-up in there, with Shazza and the TV lot. I realised I wasn't 100 per cent, but thought I'd be all right. I didn't like being the centre of everyone's attention, though. I'm used to having the camera pointed at me when I'm doing the TV job, I've been doing it enough year's now, but for some reason I hadn't even considered it was going to be like that on this record ride. The TV lot weren't holding me up, and, as usual, they couldn't do enough for me, but it was another area of my life that TV had come into. Pushbiking had always been just for me, the escape from everything. Now it wasn't.

I set off again, up to Edinburgh, then over the Forth Road Bridge. I was seeing the film crew during the day, and I knew they were only doing their job, and it was all part of it, but I kept thinking, Bugger off! They'd be following me, or right in front of me. And that's what made me realise that the loneliness was one of the reasons I loved the Tour Divide so much.

I carried on towards Dundee, and I didn't quite make the overnight stop that was on the plan. I realised if I was behind schedule by the end of day two I was going to struggle. I wasn't on song. Really, I was fucked. Because of that, and because there was always someone around that I knew, I was stopping for too long. I couldn't just get my head down.

I knew I was on the back foot before I even set off, but I wasn't selecting reverse at that point. Everything was in place. Too many people were relying on me.

A couple of days into the ride it had dawned on me that this wasn't just a case of needing to man up. The problem was I'd half finished myself at the Tour Divide, without knowing or admitting it. I thought I was the strongest I'd ever been, but I'd pushed myself preparing for the Tour Divide, doing the ride itself, and I hadn't given myself time to recover. I'd done that ride in 18 days, when the guide-book I was referring to was recommending over 70 days to do it in. Then I'd been flat out since I got home.

Another big thing was the bike. I'd been so used to pedalling my single-speed, the Rourke-framed bike I ride to work and back on, or my Tour Divide bike, but I got on this new bike and it was different. The main thing being that the cranks and pedals were slightly wider apart than I was used to and my legs just didn't like it.

I had another few hours' kip in the van, then set off again to St Andrews. On a ride like this you have to grit your teeth for the first five miles, while everything remembers what it is supposed to be doing, and, if you're fit, that's it: you're into it for the rest of the day. Because you're covering big distances, day after day, you never feel on top of the world, but before you know it you've done 50 miles. Slogging up through Scotland was different, because I couldn't escape the unforgiving pain. As I tried to compensate for the pain in my Achilles, I'd adjust my riding position and that put my knees out, which put my hips out, which put my lower back out.

At Inverness I had to stop in a bus shelter and have half an hour to myself. I'd only covered 20 miles. I wasn't right.

The weather was wet and cold, but I was dressed for it, so I wasn't feeling it. Northwave thermal winter boots, leggings over Lycra and waterproof trousers over the top, and a raincoat. The lack of daylight was a problem I hadn't thought about. But cycling in the dark for so many hours a day changes how you feel.

That night I stayed just below Wick, right in the very north of Scotland. I'd done a big chunk of riding, and I hadn't been hanging around, but that was it. The TV lot knew something wasn't right. I got up and realised, This isn't happening. The film crew had swapped back and forwards a few times. I got to John O' Groats by one in the afternoon and hated admitting I couldn't do it, but I had to tell them, This isn't happening, boys.

After what I'd put my body through that year, it was just a challenge too far. I keep saying I want to try to break myself; well, I'd just about succeeded. I was gutted I'd let myself down. I thought I had enough of a stubborn head and mental strength to get over some sore legs, but the strain on my Achilles and the repetition of tens of thousands of pedal rotations was too much. It wasn't the worst pain I've ever felt, not like slipping in the shower with a broken back or hospital porters using my broken leg to open some heavy swing doors in a Manx hospital, but it was relentless. The only time it didn't hurt was when I reached a big hill and I stood up pedalling, pushing into it.

No one at the TV company was trying to talk me into keeping going. Shazza, the one who was getting me out of bed and onto the bike at four in the morning, the one encouraging me to keep going, could tell I couldn't go on.

A lot of time and money had gone into it and there wasn't a single thing to salvage. From the TV point of view I either did it or I didn't. And I didn't. Dead simple. Plenty of the stuff we do for telly is ambitious and it doesn't always go according to plan, but we've always managed to get something out of it to make a programme, even when it was that pedal-powered boat thing that was a total failure. Not this time, though. I let everyone down.

There was plenty I know now I could've done differently. I should've had more time off. I should have had more time getting used to the new bike or just used a proven bike, that I'd done loads of miles on. I do think if I'd set off on one of my bikes, that I was used to riding, I might have been able to do it, but ifs and buts are pots and pans, and if my auntie had balls she'd be my uncle . . .

And I wouldn't do it in winter. On top of all those other excuses, the snotty cold, working like mad, New Zealand, China, Tour Divide . . . the other part was all the darkness. In Scotland I wasn't having much more than eight hours of murky daylight, and cycling in pitch black affects you. You're just not seeing anything. I thought I'd be all right, because I'd cycled up to the Strathpuffer, the far north of Scotland, in winter, and then competed in the 24-hour race, but this was different.

On the Tour Divide I could have sat down and cried my eyes out and it wouldn't have made a single bit of difference, because I was on my own. It was all on me. Shouting and screaming was just wasting energy. I just had to keep moving forward, even at 1mph; it didn't matter, I was one step closer to the finish. That was the mindset I got into in America and I couldn't get into the same mindset on the ride around Britain, because there was too much support. As good as it was, that's not why I do things like this.

With everyone heading home, me and Shazza had one night in a B&B in Inverness before driving back to

Lincolnshire and I was in a bad mood, not talking, miserable, brooding. We got home late on Saturday, I was back to work on Monday . . . I gave the pushbike a miss for a while. I could still feel the pain in my heel. I wasn't about to start running, but I could get on with stuff in the yard. Then work till Christmas. There was no point in resting now.

CHAPTER 4

'No one I knew thought it was a good idea. Not one person'

BETWEEN THE PUBLICATION of the hardback of the last book, *Worms to Catch*, and the paperback version going to print I'd been asked to write another chapter to update readers on what was happening. The final chapter of the paperback was me explaining that I was signing for Honda to race the new Fireblade. Neil Tuxworth, Honda Racing's top man in Britain, had been visiting me, planting the seed of the idea of me riding for Honda on the roads. It got the gears turning. I couldn't stop thinking, You're a long time dead, and I'd returned to the thought of not wanting any regrets when I was too old to race. I don't know what had changed from the summer, when I'd been riding from Canada to the Mexican border on my mountain bike, following the route of the Tour Divide on my own. Back then I knew I was done with serious motorbike racing. I wasn't done with bikes or racing, just the level of road racing I'd got to and the parts of it I wasn't enjoying. I was finished with it. I told everyone. I wrote it in the book. The Tour Divide made me think I should've packed in racing for teams years ago. There it was on paper.

Then there was this new 2017 Honda CBR1000RR Fireblade SP2 on Dunlops, and I thought, Fuck it, I'm going to do it. This was the very same package that John McGuinness and others had used to win races for years. I'd always be wondering, What if . . . ? if I didn't try it. No one I knew thought it was a good idea. Not one person. They all reminded me that I was so convinced when I'd come back from the Tour Divide that I'd made the right decision to pack in, but I couldn't see beyond the opportunity in front of me. And who has never changed their mind? I was in.

The road racing I'm involved with is all production bike-based. By that I mean the bikes start life as road bikes anyone can buy from a dealer. The bikes Valentino Rossi and Marc Márquez and the rest of MotoGP boys race look like TT bikes or World Superbikes, but they're pure race bikes, built in batches of two or three at a time with no parts shared with road bikes. MotoGP bikes are slightly faster around a track than racing Superbikes, that are built from a road bike, but not by much.

This is worth explaining because when a brand new road bike is released, race teams around the world have to wait for the factory to build the bikes before they can get hold of them to carry out all the changes they need to turn the road bike into a race bike and start testing. The road bike my 2017 race bikes were based on was the special edition of the regular CBR1000RR Fireblade, the Fireblade SP2. It was ready later than the regular Fireblade, so when it eventually arrived at Honda Racing's UK headquarters, in Louth, it felt like everything was happening at the eleventh hour.

There were three different levels of Fireblade in 2017. The regular one was called the CBR1000RR Fireblade. There was a fancier one, the CBR1000RR Fireblade SP, and a top of the range model, the CBR1000RR Fireblade SP2. Compared to the base model, the Fireblade SP had semi-active Öhlins suspension, different brakes, a load of electronic rider aids, a titanium petrol tank and a lighter battery. On top of that, the SP2 had a slightly different cylinder head, bigger valves and different wheels. If you went into a Honda dealer to buy the Fireblade SP2 road bike, they'd want £22,500 off you and there aren't many road bikes that are as trick.

The first chance I'd get to ride it was at a four-day test in the middle of March, which is about when I'd get on any team's bikes for the first time, so the timing wasn't a problem. What was a problem was the fact the Hondas we'd be riding weren't built into full Superbike racing specification in time for this test. That meant I'd be riding the Superstock, not the Superbike versions. These two different classes are both based on the same road bike, but the Superbike is a lot higher state of tune than the Superstock, and the rules allow a lot more modifications from the road spec, so it can take a lot longer to get the ideal settings.

The test took place at Circuito Monteblanco, near Seville, over by the southern end of the Portuguese border, a track I'd never been to. I drove down in the Transit with Francis (who smacked Nigel the dog in *When You Dead, You Dead*, if you remember). I could have flown out, but I had my Martek in the van because I was supposed to be doing a track test story with *Performance Bikes* magazine, me racing the Martek against Kawasaki's supercharged H2 road bike at the Almería circuit.

Even though Francis lost his wallet in a Spanish petrol station on the way down there, we made real good time. He was annoyed – he's a Scotsman, course he was annoyed – but we didn't have time to go back. We ended up stopping at a hotel the night before the test, a few hours' drive short of the circuit. Because I had my Martek and tools in the back of the Transit I ended up kipping on the front seat of the van while Francis stayed in the hotel. I sleep the best in my van. I loved all that and had missed that part of the racing – the road trips to testing, driving out to Spain to do a job. No bullshit, just riding plenty of laps, working with the mechanics to improve the bike, then going out on track to do it all again, riding till the tank was empty.

I'd never been to Monteblanco before, but Honda go there every year. It's cheap to rent the track, compared to other Spanish circuits, and they can do what they want there. Because they've done their pre-season testing there for a few years they know what times the previous bikes have done, so they've got a measuring stick, which is useful. Honda's world endurance and road racing boys were there: John McGuinness; Jason O'Halloran, the Australian-born British Superbike racer; Dan Linfoot; Lee Johnston and a couple of other Honda teams were sharing the test.

Like I explained, we only had the Fireblade SP2 in Superstock specification for this test, the one a lot closer to the road bike spec, but any time on the bike was handy.

I hadn't been on a race bike for 18 months and I expected it would feel like it was ripping my arms out and battering me with the messy ends for the first few laps, until I got acclimatised to a modern race bike again, but it was . . . just all right. I told my foreman in the team, Roger Smith, that I thought it was slow. He pointed at the van with my Martek in it and said, You've been riding that, haven't you? And I had, but not much, only a couple of laps on the test track. I know bikes enough and I can evaluate them pretty well, so I knew my gut feeling wouldn't be too far off.

I kept riding and loved the whole experience of being a part of the team. I loved them listening to what I was saying and me listening to what they were saying. There was no tension being in the same team as McGuinness. I might have said some things in the past that he didn't agree with and he's probably done the same, but he knows I have massive respect for him and, not just that, I like the bloke, too.

McGuinness wasn't having the best time at Monteblanco, though. He had a few issues including the front brake sticking on and nearly chucking him over the handlebars, and then I came off at the end of the first day.

I have less experience with Dunlop tyres, because most of the teams I was with had deals with Pirelli and Metzeler, and each manufacturer's tyres have different characters. Some have less ultimate grip, but when they start to slide they're more predictable, so you can keep them sliding and not feel like it's going to spit you off. Other manufacturers' tyres have more grip, but when they do eventually let go, it's a lot more sudden, harder to predict and harder to control. I didn't know where the limit of these new tyres was so I kept pushing, was trying to get a slide or summat, to let me know where the limit was, then I ended up on my ear, thinking, Oh, that's way before where I thought the limit would be.

Then McGuinness crashed, and he's not a crasher. He didn't hurt himself and he hardly marked the bike. I was new to Dunlops, but he knows them back to front and said he didn't like a particular front tyre, so we stopped using it. There are lots of different compounds (that means the recipe of the rubber; it's not rubber, but let's not get into that) and different constructions (that's how stiff the carcass of the tyre is, the carcass being the metal, Kevlar and/ or canvas that the 'rubber' tread is bonded to). Tests like this include trying new tyres out, so it wasn't too unusual. That's what testing's for.

I was enjoying being part of the team more than I was enjoying riding the bike. The quickshifter wasn't working and the blipper didn't work. You could say that's all part of the process of developing the bike, but it shouldn't really be. It's a road bike, so it should work, but there were no alarm bells; because this was Honda, it'd all be right. It took for me to get the wiring diagram out, find the quickshifter on it and say, 'Why don't we solder this wire to that wire?' to try and sort it. We got mine working and we did the same to McGuinness's. Without the quickshifter working the test is a bit pointless. This bit of kit has been used on race bikes for years and even some road bikes come with them.

The quickshifter is a sensor fastened to the gearshift pedal that cuts the ignition when it feels the rider's foot shifting gear. It means that a bike will change gear smoothly with the throttle still open. On a bike without a quickshifter you have to chop the throttle to take the pressure off the gear selector to shift smoothly. Not only is a quickshifter fractionally quicker than shifting normally, it changes so suddenly that it keeps the bike more settled on its suspension, there's less weight transfer than if you had to roll the throttle off and there's less load on the front tyre. When you're shifting down the gears, from fourth to third to second, another message from the ECU – the electronic control unit, the bike's brain – 'blips' the throttle for you to match the engine and gearbox speed. In the past riders would do it themselves, give the throttle twistgrip and a little tweak, but with advanced electronics and fuel injection the ECUs can do it for you. But the blipper wasn't working either.

So, without the quickshifter you're not testing the bike how you'd race it. It's pointless really. We were knocking the rust off, but not a lot more.

Even with these niggles I did a lot of laps, 100 a day for the four days I was there, and I felt it. There are motorbike riding muscles that I hadn't been using for a year and a half, and this was all part of the process of getting back into it.

While I was doing all those laps, I was trying to convince myself I was enjoying it, but I wasn't. I was loving sussing out wiring diagrams and soldering bits, but not the riding.

At the end of the test, we loaded up for the drive to Almería to meet *Performance Bikes* magazine for the

Martek track test. We got over the mountains, near Gibraltar, and it was pissing it down. I thought it would be all right the next day, because the track is in Tabernas, mainland Europe's only official desert region, but it wasn't. It was chucking it down again, so I got the Martek out of the van for a few photos in the car park, loaded it back up and we set off on the 24-hour drive back home. On the drive back to England I hoped I'd have the feeling that I'd really missed riding, but I didn't.

We didn't test again until Castle Combe, near Bath, on 4 and 5 April for the annual Dunlop two-day tyre test. The weather was cracking, and it was my first time on the newly completed Superbike, but I was underwhelmed again. I was thinking it was going to be something special – it was an HRC Honda Fireblade – but it felt like just another Japanese Superbike.

I made some notes in my diary: First run on the Superbike. Blipper not working. Not quick. 93 laps. McGuinness crashed on second day, dislocated thumb.

I was in the pits when he crashed, changing something on the bike, when someone told us not to go back out; something had happened. McGuinness had hurt his hand. I didn't get the chance to talk to him on the day of the crash, because he was taken off to hospital and he was still there when I set off home.

So this is two tests, two different specifications of the same bike, one Superstock, one Superbike, and all the bikes had electrical issues. Not only that, we'd had two tests and John McGuinness had crashed at both of them. I nearly crashed at Castle Combe, but didn't. It was close enough for the airbag to go off in my Dainese D-Air leathers. The gyros and processors in the leathers were so sure I was about to hit the deck that they triggered the airbag, which is around the shoulders and neck, to protect me from the imminent impact. You need a big moment to set it off. I've never done it before, or since. I was in the fast right-hander, coming on the start/finish straight, when it bucked me out of the seat.

The whole point of these tests is to push the limits and then step back from them, but the McGuinness crashes were more of a concern, because the cause of them was still a mystery.

I was back at Moody's for a couple of days at work, before McGuinness and I flew out to Japan to test the Mugen Shinden electric TT bike. Honda's official TT racers also race the Mugen in the TT Zero, the one-lap TT race for electric bikes. I'd been to Japan twice before, both times sent by *Performance Bikes* for launches of new bikes. I really like the place, partly because it feels so alien, and this visit was just the same, with the bogs that wash your arse and the people are so polite.

As soon as we landed we were taken to the Honda museum at Motegi. I was dead impressed to see that the Honda NR500 was in pride of place, because it was one of Honda's biggest failures. Honda had always been committed to four-stroke engines, but two-strokes were dominating motorcycle grand prix racing. All things being equal, and in very basic terms, a two-stroke engine can make more power because it is firing every second stroke, while a four-stroke is only firing every fourth stroke. By this era bikes were limited to a maximum of four cylinders and an upper cylinder capacity of 500cc, so Honda came up with the idea of making odd-shaped pistons, what all the British magazines described as being the shape of a Spam tin. The idea was to increase the valve area of a 500cc engine. Bigger valves can pass more air and fuel into the combustion chamber and can make more power. Combine that with higher revs and they might make a four-stroke engine that can compete with a two-stroke.

The bike was a disaster, its results were terrible, it was unreliable. It was too ambitious, but it was brave. And here it was, right in the middle of the corporate museum. I took that to mean that Honda had learned loads by failing and were proud of trying. And I liked that.

This wasn't a big part of me joining Honda, but getting to race the Mugen Shinden was definitely a bonus. It has been developed by Mugen, but it's closely related to Honda. I tested the bike on track. It's a beautiful piece of kit, and fast, but it is heavy, weighing 248kg, where the minimum weight limit of a Superbike is 168kg. It weighs so much because of all of the lithium-ion batteries it needs to shift as fast as it does.

McGuinness was still suffering with his dislocated thumb, so he hardly rode the Mugen in Japan, but he knew the bike inside out because he'd raced it a few times at the TT already. All that had changed from the bike he'd raced the previous year was a new front mudguard and how quickly the battery could charge. They hoped the mudguard would make some aerodynamic improvements, but it was hard to tell because we were testing it at a go-kart track.

Back home there were plenty of tests arranged for me on the Superbike, so there was no lack of time on the bike or lack of effort from Honda Racing. The next test was at the Oulton Park race track, Cheshire, where I stopped off on my way to the Tandragee 100 road races near Portadown, Co. Armagh, Northern Ireland, being held on 21–2 April. I tested the Superbike at Oulton, but I would race the Super-stocker at Tandragee.

One of the reasons I went back to Tandragee was because I didn't race the TT in 2016. I was cycling through America on the Tour Divide instead. If it's either your first year at the TT, or you missed a year, you have to get signatures on your race licence to be given a start permission for the TT. This is what everyone is supposed to do to prove they've got enough experience to race there. Of course, it doesn't guarantee safety, and the TT and the ACU (the Auto-Cycle Union) know I knew my way around the place. Also, because I was racing for the official Honda team it would only need a phone call to get me permission, but I didn't want to owe any favours or be open to anyone coming back and saying, 'Well, we broke the rules to get you your start permission, so can you just . . . ?' I wanted to tick all the boxes and get all my signatures, six of them, to show six national level finishes, between the end of one TT and the start of the next. I already had one from New Zealand, where I'd raced in November 2016 on my Martek, so the races I chose were Tandragee, Cookstown, Scarborough, and two races from the North West, because there are two different race days.

At this stage, six weeks before the TT, the team still weren't 100 per cent sure they had fixed what had caused McGuinness's Castle Combe crash. Nothing had been mentioned publicly, and never would be – until now – but the team told me they wanted to check a few things before I competed at Tandragee, which would be the first real road race the 2017 Fireblade SP2 would take part in. I knew what they were really doing: checking it wasn't likely to spit me off into a field.

It's worth explaining that the 2017 Honda Fireblade, like lots of modern bikes, has what they call a ride-by-wire throttle. What that means is there is no mechanical link between the twistgrip throttle, that the rider twists back and forward to increase or decrease the revs of the bike, and the fuel injection system. For most of the previous hundred and whatever years of the history of motorcycles, there's been a cable, or two, between the throttle and the carb or fuel-injection throttle bodies. It's a mechanical connection between the rider's hand and the fuel system.

With ride-by-wire systems, the twistgrip looks the same, and feels the same, but instead of cable there's a potentiometer that measures the movement of the grip and sends an electrical signal, via the ECU, to a stepper motor that opens and closes the throttle bodies. The reason for this extra complication, compared to a cable, is that modern fuel-injection systems can work more closely with all the new, more sophisticated traction control and wheelie control systems.

Modern fuel systems can overrule what the rider is asking for to deliver a smoother and safer ride for road riders and racers. But there is also the possibility of the motorcycle overthinking or misinterpreting what the rider wants. This meant there was a question mark over what the ride-by-wire throttle was doing.

The throttle takes a lot into account. When the bike feels the rider's foot changing down a gear, the ECU automatically 'blips' the throttle; it acts like the rider giving the twistgrip a short, sharp turn. It does this to load and unload the gearbox's dogs, the meshing gear teeth, momentarily for a smoother gear change. Some sportscars do it automatically. Before these electronic blippers, riders would do it themselves, while on the brakes into a corner. The engine knows, in the time of that blip, the gear selector barrel should move from third to second, or whatever gear, but it doesn't just see third gear and second gear, it knows every increment in between. It sounded to me that when McGuinness had crashed and dislocated his thumb he was going down the gears to enter a corner, and the gear hadn't fully engaged, so it had kept blipping. He'd closed the throttle, but the ECU had kept it open while he had the bike leant over, and he'd lost the front end. Like anyone would. It was a really clever system, but the program needed rewriting so it couldn't happen again.

I was given the all-clear to race, so I set off for Ireland. Someone told me I hadn't raced at Tandragee since 2005 and when I got there I couldn't work out why it had been so long. It's the most hardcore road race of the lot. It's amazing and the kind of track I love racing on.

Practice was Friday 21 April, the race the next day. The races in Northern Ireland are different to most of those elsewhere in the world, because they don't race on Sundays out of respect to the religious.

Even though I loved the whole event, and being back on the Irish roads, I struggled. I can't even tell you where I finished, but I was off the pace. I bet people thought it was because I'd had a year off from racing, but it wasn't.

After Tandragee I got a ferry out of Belfast at eleven that Saturday evening, drove through the night and got to Scarborough at six in the morning for the Scarborough Spring National Cup as well. I was doing loads of riding. No one could accuse me of not putting in the hours in the saddle.

My results at the two Irish races and Scarborough were terrible. Bloody terrible. McGuinness hadn't competed at those races – he very rarely did – and it never usually affected his performance; he'd been the man to beat for years. Everyone who wanted to do well at the TT always raced the North West 200 in Northern Ireland, a couple of weeks before the start of the TT. It's never been a favourite of mine, but I've done all right there over the years. I'd talked myself into feeling optimistic about the 2017 race, but that didn't last long.

CHAPTER 5

'Killing myself, that would be a failure'

BY NOW IT was the middle of May, meaning the TT's practice week started in less than three weeks and it was time for the North West 200. On my way through Lancashire I picked up Cammy – Cameron Whitworth – who has been my mechanic in loads of teams going right back to AIM Yamaha in 2006, and had been involved with a couple of telly shows, including Pikes Peak. He was now working for William Dunlop for the season, and we got the ferry over to Northern Ireland. I was staying at my mate Paul's in Ballymoney, so I was just in the paddock when I needed to be. I had a Triumph Tiger road bike in the back of my van, so I could get from Paul's house to the pits, but Honda weren't keen on me turning up on a Triumph, so I ended up parking it at the other end of the pits and putting a bit of gaffer tape on the tank that I wrote 'Africa Triple' on, because Honda build an Africa Twin.

When I first visited the team's awning, McGuinness and I were talking to the team about the issues we were both having with the bikes: the quickshifter and the more worryingly blipper problem that had caused John to crash at the Castle Combe test. We weren't hiding anything from them. Why would we? I did get the feeling that the team thought I was rusty and that was the root of the problem. Plenty of people were saying that, but I was happy to keep my mouth shut and let them think whatever they wanted.

We were both struggling with a throttle connection problem, too, but McGuinness thought the new bike was fast in some situations, where I was pretty sure it wasn't. All you had to do was look at the speed trap times at the North West to see we were miles off, summat like 15mph down. Agreed, you're not on full throttle for long, but that deficit takes some making up, and if the bike's not doing what you want on corner entry you haven't got a chance.

On Thursday night, 11 May, we went out for qualifying on the Superbikes. On a flying lap, McGuinness crossed the finish line to start another timed lap, went through the first fast right, called Millbank, and into the fast left, Primrose Hill, and crashed.

He slid up the road and hit the railings between the path at the side of the road and the golf course that's right on the coast there. It was a big one. He broke his right leg, four vertebrae and some ribs.

He must have broken his leg fairly early on in the accident, because he lost 50mm of bone on the road as it ground away. Later in the year they gave him a bone graft and put on an external fixator frame, like Ian Hutchinson had for so long after his bad accident at Silverstone in 2010. They've got some length back in McGuinness's leg, but it was properly buggered. I went to see him in hospital and he was talking sense, but he was fucked.

He told me he'd shut the throttle to go down a gear and the bike behaved like he'd opened it. Looking back, I do wonder if it didn't happen to me because I'm more aggressive with the gear lever than McGuinness. Perhaps I really stamp on it, relatively speaking, so the bike's gear position sensor is in no doubt that I'm changing gear. Perhaps that's why he had the problem twice and I never had it.

McGuinness was still very Honda, the company man, even to me. I didn't need anyone to give me advice at that point. I knew what I was doing and what I was thinking. I will often ask, 'What do you think?', but I know what I'm doing, so what am I asking you for?

Honda decided to withdraw from the North West 200, with the new team manager, Jonny Twelvetrees, saying, 'We now need to determine what happened and will sit out the Superstock and Superbike races, get back to Louth to analyse John's bike and regroup ahead of our next test at Castle Combe in a couple of weeks before we head to the Isle of Man.'

Honda Racing were just competing with the 1000cc bikes, so I'd agreed to race Wilson Craig's Honda 600s in the Supersport class at the North West and the TT. I still ended up racing his 600s, so I got enough signatures on my licence to race at the TT. I'd raced with Wilson in 2010, the year *TT3D: Closer to the Edge* had been filmed, and I liked the bloke, and the bikes were good, but because the focus was on trying to sort the big bikes I wasn't giving the 600s as much time as I would have liked to and I wasn't doing them, or myself, justice in the 600 races. If things are going according to plan you can put in good times in different classes, but if you're trying to sort out big problems with one bike and that's where you've decided your focus should be, the other class is compromised.

There's two weeks between the end of the North West and the start of the TT's practice week and things weren't looking great. If anything, though, I felt the pressure was off me – the bike's tried to kill my teammate. I'm shrugging and thinking, you can't blame me, but that's not my attitude normally.

Even before John's crash, and Honda pulling out of the North West, it was obvious to me that the bike was just so slow and it wouldn't do what I wanted it to. A perfect example of this was on corner entry: it wasn't decelerating into corners like I wanted it to. It didn't have the aggressive engine braking a big Superbike should have when I shut the throttle. I wanted it to close the throttle hard to transfer the weight onto the front tyre so I could throw it into the corner how I wanted it to. There was a fraction of a second delay every time I asked it to do anything because the bike's ECU was taking so many things into account (or that's what I put it down to), and, because of that, it wasn't giving me the outright control I wanted and needed. I wanted it to react to everything my hand did. I wasn't asking for the impossible. I'd been racing bikes on the roads for ten years and they'd all given me the response I wanted and expected, so it wasn't some unobtainable goal. Hour-long races are regularly won and lost by a couple of seconds, so if you're just 1 per cent off the pace you're nowhere.

I got back from the North West at three in the morning on 14 May and I'd been thinking about the bike all the way home. I suggested an extra test to the team. I was willing to race the bike, even though no one was sure if the problem had been solved, or even what the cause was, but the lack of top speed was more of an issue when we'd sorted all the other problems out. I never wanted to just make up the numbers, but if the bike wasn't quick enough, it didn't matter what I did, that's all I was ever going to be doing.

After a week working at Moody's I went to Elvington on Saturday to meet the team. Elvington is an airfield, to the south-east of York, that holds motorcycle top-speed and sprint events, and has done for years. The idea was to get out on the runway, that's nearly two miles long, and just see what the 2017 Fireblade SP2 would do flat out, in a straight line in ideal conditions. I'd decided that if it couldn't do 200mph on an airfield there was no point in even going to the TT.

We turned up in a couple of vans, no fuss, and lined up for some top-speed runs on the official Honda Racing Superbike. Tucked in, flat out, I was clocked at 187mph, then 192mph on my next run. BMW S1000RR road bikes were doing 202mph. I was on a 230-horsepower Super-bike, but it wouldn't do 200. Roger, from the Honda team, said, 'It's very rare that you do 200mph at the TT,' which is true, but you've got to have the ability to do it. The 200mph target was just a line in the sand. I believed if it didn't do it, it couldn't possibly be competitive.

And this wasn't me looking for excuses; it came off the back of the poor speed trap readings we'd already had in races. Testing it on the airfield took any doubt out of the job. No one could say, 'Well, it was the rider not twisting the throttle, or not getting out of the previous corner as quick as the boys he's racing.' No, this was as close to labo-ratory conditions as we could get and it was being beaten by older Fireblades with nothing but new exhausts and a remaps.

I told Roger, 'You can see the data, you can see I'm flat on the throttle, you can see I'm tucked in, you can see the bike's flat out, if it can't do 200mph what's the point?'

But I went to the TT anyway . . .

If this had been a privateer Honda team, not the usual Honda set-up, I would have been begging to use the previous year's bike, but there was no possibility of that with the official team. It would be more of a PR disaster.

Meanwhile, Honda Racing had asked a few lads to stand in for McGuinness on the factory Honda. This is what normally happens if a top team's rider is injured before the TT and usually there isn't a problem filling the seat. I heard the team asked Lee Johnston and Cameron Donald and they both turned them down. These lads, who were without rides for various reasons – Lee because he'd left his team, Cam because he'd retired – were turning down the chance of a factory Honda TT ride. What was that saying about the bike, its chances and its reputation in the paddock? Anyone who knew, knew what it had done to McGuinness, but I was still there.

I went to see McGuinness again on the Friday night before I caught the ferry to the Isle of Man. He lives just down the road from where I was getting the boat at Heysham. I wasn't after any words of wisdom, or anything like that, I just wanted to see how he was. His leg was a right mess and he just reminded me I had nothing to prove, make sure you come home in one piece.

First practice was supposed to be Saturday, but it was cancelled because of low cloud. Sunday I tested the Mugen at Jurby. Monday there wasn't any practice. I only did eight laps in practice, before the first race. Wilson Craig's 600 was good, but I hadn't had any time on it. Because of the weather we hardly had any practice time, and maybe I should have concentrated on getting that Supersport 600 right and making the best of a bad job, but I persevered with the Superbike instead, thinking it was the most important.

The TT races take place over two weeks. There are practice sessions every day of the first week, practice week, and race week starts on the middle Saturday, with the Superbike TT, weather permitting. It hardly needs saying I wasn't full of confidence, but I was still going to give it my best. I set off from the start, and was just over seven miles into the first lap of a 227-mile race, going into Doran's Bend, a fast left-hander you have to commit to if you're going to get round it at racing speed. The lead up to it is fifth gear, on a Superbike, and even one that isn't capable of race-winning pace, it's still the thick end of 160mph, then you're braking and going down the box to take the bend at about 110mph. I shifted down to the fourth and the bike went into a false neutral.

Going into this very fast-left-hander, like any corner, you use the bike's engine braking to help you make the corner. If the bike jumps into neutral, there is no engine braking and the bike doesn't behave like you want it to. It should be slowing as it engages a lower gear, but it's coasting and feels like it's accelerating. I'm still fighting it to turn, but it feels like it wants to go straight on while I'm trying to find a gear, pressing the gear lever, and nothing's happening, so I commit to making the corner before I run out of road. I'm leant right over and run up the kerb, then run up the side of the wall and slide off the bike. Committing to the corner and not panicking saved my bacon. All that was on my mind was, Try to get round, try to get round. If I'd have panicked and gone straight on, I'd be brown bread.

I ended up on the inside of the bend, the bike on the kerb of the outside. I jumped to my feet and legged it off the road, because another bike, with Peter Hickman, was seconds behind me.

The cool head that had saved my skin on more than one occasion disappeared and as soon as I stood up I was shouting at the bike. It was destroyed but I was reminding it what it had done to John McGuinness and what it had tried to do to me. A second or so later I was trying to pick it up and onto the pavement, with the help of the marshals. From me losing the front to picking it up was 20 seconds.

Hitting a false neutral happens, and I've had them with Hondas before, but this wasn't pilot error. In 2009 we had gearbox problems (when I was with Shaun Muir's private Honda team). We had no spare parts, but the factory team brought one for us and Cammy, my mechanic, put it in. This was nothing to do with the problem that caused McGuinness's crash; it was just one of those things, maybe a slightly worn part in the gearbox.

I hurt my wrist and it shook me up. If you saw the interviews that went out on the telly the same night you could see I wasn't myself.

So that was the first race of three that the Fireblade SP2 could enter that TT. The next race was the Superstock 1000 race, followed by the big one, Senior. The SP2 can race in all three classes, but it's a different specification for the Superstock race. The front suspension can be modified but not changed from the road bike spec that anyone can buy. The Superstocks have less sophisticated engine management systems than the Superbikes are allowed, but that's less of a problem now, because the road bike systems the race bikes are based on are all-singing, all-dancing now anyway, with anti-wheelie, launch control and traction control as standard. The Superstocker is also a lower state of tune that the Superbike, meaning it's less powerful, but Superstock BMWs can still easily break 200mph at the TT, on a two-way road that's open to the public every day of the year.

I wasn't really talking to Neil Tuxworth at this stage. There was no falling out, but my day-to-day points of contact were Jonny Twelvetrees and Roger Smith. Twelvetrees was introduced to the press as the Honda race team manager, Tuxworth's replacement. Big shoes to fill. It seemed to me that Tuxworth was still watching everything that was going on, but he was definitely less hands on.

Jonny Twelvetrees is the older brother of the England rugby player, Billy, and had a very pragmatic approach to the motorbike job. Jonny is a nice bloke, perhaps too human for road racing. I think the experience of the TT and what's at stake rattled him and he didn't want anything to do with the place, because he knew what could happen. It's sport, but lives are at risk.

There were times when other team managers would make it clear: We pay your wage, you get on it, and Twelvetrees didn't want to say that. Tuxworth would. So, in a strange way, I had more respect for Tuxworth, because he was more businesslike. I'm not saying he'd send you to your death, but he explains things in a very rational way, that would make me think, Oh yeah, I should just get on and ride it. Not that anyone put me under pressure to ride it; the team were brilliant. Part of me thinks they should have just manned up and told me to get on with it. I was being a bit woolly about the job. I was thinking, It's tried to kill my teammate, it's just chucked me off, fuck that!

Then Honda race team's management confirmed they were withdrawing the Superstock-spec Fireblade SP2, because of the question marks over the electronics, so I had even less time on the track. At that point I was still planning to race the Superbike-spec Fireblade SP2.

Andy Spellman was over for the whole two weeks and he couldn't understand why I was still willing to race it. I make my own decisions, but he helps if he can, and sorts out stuff that I don't want to get involved in, which is bloody handy sometimes. It wasn't me not manning up to the job, but I was so close to the situation, maybe I couldn't see it clearly. I don't like letting people down and wouldn't criticise the team that I needed to trust, I was there to do a job until someone told me I couldn't. Spellman was going into meetings with Honda telling them that he believed Honda had a moral obligation not to put me on a bike they couldn't guarantee was safe. He's very knowledgeable about motorsport, but he was looking at it from a different point of view to TT people, and he certainly wasn't alone.

I had Sharon and both the dogs with me. She wasn't keen on me going back to racing, but she knew why I was and left it up to me. We stayed at my mate Gary's near Ginger Hall and I love it there, but the atmosphere was tense in the Honda pit.

I appreciated that everyone was concerned about me and telling me why I shouldn't get back on the bike, but I had my Tour Divide head on, the single-minded determination to get my head down and get on with it.

Everything was pointing to packing it in, not getting back on the bike, but I saw that walking away would be the same as giving in and I don't do that if I can help it. I'm not a giving-in person.

Before the Senior, if conditions allow, the race organisers permit the riders who are going to compete in the final race of the TT one last practice lap each. I went out on the Superbike-spec Fireblade, and if they'd have pulled me in after half a lap I'd have said, Bugger it, we'll race it, that bike's all right now, good enough to race, it's the best it's been. We can do something with this. But the session didn't end after half a lap and as I got around to the 33rd, the corner on the track that marks the 33rd mile of the 37.73-mile course, I came across all this mist in the air. It turned out to be oil from, I'm guessing, a blown engine, and I nearly come off on oil dropped on the road.

As soon as I could, I stopped next to some marshals and was shouting and screaming at them that something was on the track and telling them to get some flags out, to warn riders. As I was setting off, I looked over my shoulder and saw something happening, a bike going down. Someone hadn't been as lucky as I'd been.

It's less than five miles back to the pits from where I hit the oil and I was angry when I pulled into the pit lane. I was telling my mechanics there should've been flags out. Then we were told the practice session had been red-flagged, stopped immediately. What I'd seen over my shoulder was the lad behind me, a 33-year-old Irish rider called Alan Bonner. He came off on the dropped oil and died as a result of his injuries. According to those who tot these things up, he was the 255th competitor to die on the

TT's current Mountain course since 1911 and the third in two days. Jochem van den Hoek didn't survive his accident at the 11th Milestone earlier that day and Davey Lambert died after crashing at Greeba Castle the day before. That was it, I was off home. I never normally think, That could've been me. It's pointless, it wasn't me, but I couldn't help it this time. The crash I survived earlier in the week felt like I'd got away with a big one. I'd pushed my luck enough for one race meeting.

Spellman pointed out that even after all that had happened they still wanted me to race that bike and the ball was in my court. I had to be the one to say I wasn't willing to. All week he'd been saying it should've have been the team who pulled the bike and take the decision out of my hands.

He went to see Honda and sat with them to finalise the press release that would announce I wasn't going to compete in the Senior. All the big bods were in there, including Honda UK's top man. Spellman said he was dead calm, there were no arguments and he just delivered his view on what he'd seen during the previous 13 days. He told them the bike wasn't developed or competitive and maybe not even safe and that it should be seen as a team decision to withdraw from the Senior, with no blame. If the press release was going to say it was my decision then I should have the right to say why I pulled out. He reckoned they couldn't have it both ways. Honda wanted to say that I'd withdrawn from the Senior, which was true, but the reasons I did it for I wasn't allowed to say.

Spellman had talked to Jonny Twelvetrees before and felt like he was going over old ground again, but he reminded them that a rider like me could bang in 127s on any big bike in the paddock, but without McGuinness here there was no way to prove that the Blade was not fast enough, so it was easy to say I wasn't pushing it as I was rusty. He also pointed out, again, that I'd gone nearly as quick as a newcomer in 2004 with no TT experience, on a bike I'd built with my dad, so having a year out wasn't an excuse for the times.

The lack of practice didn't help, and I wasn't at my fastest, but the bike was holding me back, I wasn't holding it back. Dean Harrison passed me in the Superbike race within four miles of the start, like I was stood still and I was pushing.

It was all going back and forth. The team said their data showed I'd been on the back brake down Bray Hill, to which Spellman said no doubt because the bike wasn't stable and that proved it needed development. They argued it didn't need developing; it was just my riding style and requirements were different to John's and the bike was quicker and faster than the previous year's bike, and that I wasn't getting the best out of it and needed more bike and riding time.

I wasn't at this meeting, but the way he explained it was like something from a courtroom drama. They'd say something and Spellman would come back with a counter-argument. After they told him I just needed to ride the bike more, he asked why I didn't I have a stock bike to ride, like plenty of other riders in the Superbike class. They said because they wanted to concentrate on getting the Superbike right for me. 'So he's developing it then?' Spellman asked. 'Because you're not developing it with any logic because you've got a stock gearbox and an engine out of the BSB bike. If you're concentrating on the Superbike why let Guy out on the Wilson Craig Supersport? If that's so he can get more laps, then why not run the stocker?'

He wanted to make it clear that, for whatever reason, the bike wasn't ready to race at the sharp end of a TT and had problems that we, as a team, couldn't put our fingers on. But they wouldn't have it that their bikes weren't suitable or competitive and it was my riding that was at fault. One of the bigwigs poked his head up from his computer and said. 'There's two truths to this story.' So Spellman asked, 'Was John happy with the bike then?' knowing that testing hadn't gone well for either of us. One of the main men said, 'Yes, he said it was faster and better all round than last year's.'

Spellman may not be technically minded but he can smell the bullshit a mile off and when you know the truth and someone is telling you the opposite and trying to dress it up in technical data, then you know they're really saying 'We agree but the boss is sat here and I've got a steady job, thank you.'

Honda told Spellman they were still keen for me to compete at Southern 100 and Ulster GP, races I love and have had plenty of success at, but when he asked if there were tests planned he was told by Jonny Twelvetrees, 'I'm going to turn my phone off and get away from motorbikes for a few weeks.'

He came back to the van, pulled me aside and told me, 'You can't trust a team that won't see the wood for the trees', then relayed all of the above and more. He reckoned if I took the name Honda off that bike I would look at it differently.

Spellman normally stays out of team business, but he was saying this was about facts and revealing what the team were really thinking and saying out loud. I read the statement they'd hammered out and I was happy with it. I thought it was very diplomatic. Honda blamed the weather for a lack of track time and that I'd made the decision, because we weren't doing the lap times to be competitive. There was no finger-pointing. Those that knew, knew what was going on. If others thought it was all down to me, it was no skin off my nose.

As we were talking, one of Honda's PR blokes, who Spellman had argued with earlier in the week, rang him. Spellman put his finger to his lips to tell me and Sharon to be quiet, and put his phone on speaker so I could hear him. The PR bloke questioned one word on the press statement that was going out with my name on. It didn't sound right apparently.

Now, I'd been really calm up to that point but you could call it good timing or bad that he called up . . . I interrupted him and said, 'All right, mate. It's Guy here . . .' Then I let rip. I reminded him that I could have told people what I really thought of the bike, but I wasn't doing that, but don't twist it even more.

I shouted, 'Do you want me to tell all these cameras and people that your motorbike tried to kill my teammate and me?' I was on the limiter. I kept repeating, 'Is that what you want, mate? Is it, is it?' I was shaking a bit, still, and Spellman calmly said, 'I think they know what you really think now. That's cleared the air.'

I then felt myself get Brian the Chimp back under control and started to laugh. I was a bit embarrassed really and said so to Spellman and Shazza, but after those two weeks I felt a lot better for letting rip.

Spellman then had another call and was very calm; we played the game, were professional and out went the statement to the press and public, but we were all a little wiser.

Even then I was still thinking about the Ulster Grand Prix, and after the TT I tested the Fireblade at Cadwell Park in Lincolnshire, but that proved to be just one final confirmation that I'd made up my mind.

In late July 2017 Honda released a statement, saying, 'Having extracted and reviewed the data from the ECU on John's bike, we now know that a setting on the ECU race kit software resulted in the throttle blipping unexpectedly . . .

'Although at the time there was a long delay in getting the data from John's bike due to the ECU being damaged – the ECU had to be sent all the way to the supplier in China to extract the data from it – we put in a counter-measure of a new spec of ECU for the TT to ensure the problem wouldn't happen again.'

Looking back at what I wrote in February 2017, before I'd even ridden the new Fireblade, is interesting. 'The target is to do the best I can do. Of course I want to win, but I just want to go back and ride. What would be a failure? Killing myself, that would be a failure. Anything other than that is a result. Win, lose or draw, I want to be getting off the bike and saying, I couldn't have done any more, I had control for all the race.'

I was right when I finished the Tour Divide in 2016. I was done with racing at this level. Not done with motorbikes or even racing motorbikes, but trying to win TTs.

I wasn't looking at the TAS team that I'd been with the last time I'd raced the TT and seeing them doing the winning with any jealousy. I walked away from the experience so I had no regrets about any of it. I could've been laid in a box thinking, 'You berk! Why did I do that? I told you so, you dickhead.' But I got a second bite of the cherry and no harm done.

CHAPTER 6

'The last thing I needed to be doing was chucking that thing down the road. It cost £450,000'

PART OF SIGNING to race for Honda on the roads, after all I'd said about not going back, was being given the opportunity to ride the legendary Honda Six.

This bike, that Honda built for the 1967 season and named the RC174, was a development of the original Honda six-cylinder GP bike, the 250cc RC164, that made its racing debut in the summer of 1964. Back then the rules weren't as tight as they are now, so engineers and factories could really use their imaginations to solve problems and improve the breed.

Each racing class was, as they are now, limited by an upper cylinder capacity, so Mr Honda and his engineers decided they would make more power by increasing the rev limit their bikes could safely reach. This is where it gets a bit more complicated. The upper limit of what an engine will rev to is governed by a bunch of different factors, but the main one is the mass of the piston and the length of the stroke; both these relate to the speed the piston can travel at. It's possible for a single-cylinder 250cc bike to have almost countless different bore and stroke dimensions to reach the 250cc displacement, but there is a balance between the size and mass of the piston, and the stroke and how that relates to the speed the piston travels that naturally governs how fast it can move.

Successful British racing bikes of the 1950s and early 1960s, like the 500cc Manx Norton and AJS 7R, were simple and effective singles, but they were often outgunned by much more complicated, and more expensive, Italian multi-cylinder bikes like the MV Agusta triple. The Italian triple could rev higher and make more power for a given cylinder capacity. There are downsides to multi-cylinder bikes, but when they're good, they have the advantage over singles.

Honda took the idea of multi-cylinder bikes to extremes. They built a 250cc twin, then a four-cylinder 250 and a 50cc twin, back when that was still a GP class. They also built a five-cylinder 125, called the RC148, in 1965 to compete against Suzuki's two-strokes. The Honda 125 revved to 22,000rpm and its most famous racer, Luigi Taveri, reckoned he had to keep it revving between 21,000 and 22,000rpm to get the most out of it. Remember, rpm means revs per minute. Each of the tiny little pistons are going up and down 360 times per second! A modern Super-bike, like the Honda Fireblade SP2, revs to about 13,000rpm. Honda's five-cylinder 125 is a very underrated motorbike.

In the mid-sixties Honda had their hands full in the 250 class with Phil Read on the Yamaha two-stroke. The multi-cylinder solution had worked in the 50 and 125 classes, and Taveri was world champion on the five-cylinder 125 in 1966. Honda already had a four-cylinder 250, but it wasn't fast enough, so they started developing a six-cylinder 250 in January 1964. They weren't hanging about. They had an engine running in June of that year and were racing the finished bike just two months later.

Time was so tight that to get it from Japan to its first race, at Monza in Italy, Honda paid for three seats on the plane from Japan, then arranged with the airline to take the row out so that the bike could fit there because they couldn't guarantee there would be room in the hold. When it arrived in Italy, Jim Redman, the rider who had convinced Honda to debut it at that race, pushed it out of the plane, down the steps and through customs! He led the race, this amazing, revolutionary bike's first race, but it overheated and Redman ended up third.

By 1966 Honda had signed Mike Hailwood for his first full season on the bike, the best rider in the world at the time, perhaps ever. Together they beat the two-strokes to the 250 title.

Honda were also competing in the 350cc grand prix series, with a four-cylinder, but the smaller six was quicker than it. So they increased the size of the bore to make the 297cc 1967 RC174 that could race in the important 350 class. Hailwood won the 350 title, too.

My Honda Six ride was set for a Sunday in June at Castle Combe race circuit near Bath. I'd raced the Krazy Horse Harley chopper at DirtQuake, at King's Lynn, the day before and as soon as I was done there, me and Shazza drove down to near Castle Combe, where we'd been booked to stay in the poshest hotel. We met up with Neil Tuxworth and his missus, and George Beale, whose bike I was going to ride, and his missus. The next morning we had breakfast, no rushing about; drove to the track and found we had a place to have a quiet cup of tea. I was already thinking, This is amazing.

Then I saw the bike. I already knew is wasn't the actual RC174 that Hailwood had raced in the 1960s; only two were ever made, and two spare engines, but it's an exact replica that George Beale had made. Even so that didn't take any of the gloss off riding it. George is a right interesting and dead knowledgeable bloke. He'd run GP teams in the 1970s and 1980s, sponsored dozens of riders and was Barry Sheene's team manager for a while. He'd been a bike dealer; bought and sold rare racing bikes; is a consultant to specialist auction houses and has made a business out of making replicas of amazing old race bikes. He started in the early seventies when he needed a part for the AJS 7R he owned. He needed an exhaust and you couldn't buy one, so he went to a company in Birmingham, the only people he could find who could make a perfect replica. But they wouldn't make just one; they had a minimum order of 50. George must have really wanted that exhaust, because he ordered 50 and started selling them. People asked him for other parts and he realised there was a market, and he ended up making so many parts that, in the end, he started building complete 7R replicas.

He made replicas of other racing bikes, like the Italian Benelli, and was visited by a mate of his who ran Honda's official museum. He asked George, 'Do you fancy building a replica Six?' And that's how it came about. Honda not only gave him permission to copy their bike, they bought the first replica from him.

When it was nearly time for my go on the bike I got my black leathers on and walked over to where the bike would be started and warmed up. George and Neil Tuxworth were my mechanics for the day. As soon as it came to life I was sure nothing had ever sounded more violent than a Honda Six. When the bike is running the springs in the carbs aren't strong enough to push the slides back, so when you let go of the throttle it just sits at those revs. You have to physically close the throttle.

It is only 297cc and makes 66 horsepower, about a third of what a modern TT Superbike makes, but it's bloody intimidating when you hear it being warmed up. I made sure I had earplugs in.

The bike has absolute instant throttle response. There's nothing else like it. The revs rise and fall so fast as the six individual exhaust pipes bark a noise that I've never heard a motorcycle make before. You think it's a normal classic when it's on a steady throttle, but as soon as you rev it you realise there's nothing normal about this engine. It's a sound I'll never forget.

Then it was time to ride the Honda. The components in the engine are so tiny, valves like roofing nails, but it didn't feel like it's made of watch parts. The riding position is cramped. I couldn't believe they could get six cylinders into such a small space.

One of the downsides of making power from increasing the rpm of an engine, which is what these Hondas were all about, was the engine has what's called a narrow powerband. That's nothing physical, it means the engine only makes its peak power in a very limited rev range. If you've never ridden a motorbike with a narrow powerband, the easiest way to explain the feeling is this: when you're driving up a hill and the car begins to slow down and the engine revs drop, you know you've got to shift down a gear to get the engine spinning and making more power again. Drop it a gear and you begin to accelerate again. When the car slows down, it's dropped out of the powerband; by changing gear you're allowing the engine to start spinning and making power again.

These little multi-cylinder motorbikes had such narrow powerbands that they needed very close-ratio gearboxes to keep them spinning without losing too many revs. The Honda Six has a seven-speed gearbox to compensate. I was up and down the gearbox like a fiddler's elbow to keep it in the powerband and I was only having a fairly gentle ride round. Going into Tower Bend I would normally go down two gears on a Superbike, but I was going back five on the Honda. It was designed to rev to 17,000rpm, but George said it would be better not to rev it above 16,000, so I made sure I didn't.

Honda didn't have any drawings for the engine, so when George came to tool up to make the replicas he used a French firm called JPX who specialise in aircraft and F1 engines; they said it was the most difficult engine they'd ever seen, and it was made in the mid-sixties! JPX made over 500 drawings of components. There are three different sizes of conrod big ends in the same engine and seven different main bearings. The tiny pistons, just 41mm in diameter, are machined from solid. To make a set of six carbs cost £18,000 twenty years ago.

Take the noise and the numbers on the rev counter out of it and it wasn't that different to riding a normal motorbike, but it's hard to ignore the noise and the numbers.

When I was on track I wasn't pushing it, I was just riding it. I'm not a showman, but I could imagine that people were there to hear that bike. I would travel to hear it, so I made sure I was revving it as hard as George would let me.

I did five laps before I could feel oil on my boot and it was causing my foot to slip on the peg. If it was going on the peg I knew there was a good chance it was going on the back tyre and had an oil leak, so I came in. The last thing I needed to be doing was chucking that thing down the road. There are only six in the world, and if you want one they cost over £450,000. When I looked there *was* oil on the tyre.

The oil was being blown out of the breather box. George explained they had a problem with early four-strokes, but he's sorted it since I rode it. When I went out again it was still blowing oil, so I only had eight laps in total, but it was still a great experience.

The Honda Sixes were Mike Hailwood's favourite racing motorbikes because they were so easy to win on. It was the most amazing bike I'd ever ridden. It makes 74 horsepower, has four tiny valves per cylinder, and six individual carburettors.

There are only a handful of bikes I'd put on a list of those I would love the chance to ride: the Britten, the Honda Six and Steve Burns's Monster – the turbocharged Spondon Suzuki that I read about in *Performance Bikes* magazine when I was a lad. Those are the benchmark motorbikes for me. There are fantastic racing motorbikes, like the Honda NSR500 and the RC211V, but there was nothing particularly groundbreaking about them. I would possibly add the Honda NR500 to the list, the oval-piston grand prix four-stroke that I'd seen at Honda's Motegi museum.

If I had to rate them, I'd say George's Honda Six was better than the Britten, which is a bold statement. The Britten, that I rode in New Zealand, was like nothing else, and so strange to ride because of its handling characteristics, but the Honda Six felt like a conventional motorcycle, just more extreme. How it revs, how narrow it is, how light it is, how close the gearbox ratios are, how fast it accelerates for a 55-year-old 297cc motorbike.

The Honda Six, the five-cylinder 125 and the twin-cylinder 50, with its 12-speed gearbox and four valves per cylinder, were all amazing. You don't see anything like that any more. All the rules are made to homogenise the bikes, and cars, to control costs, except for rare races like the Pikes Peak Hill Climb, the Time Attack series for four-wheelers, and machines competing at places like Bon-neville. I'm not dismissing the work of the engineers in MotoGP or F1, because they're exploring marginal gains to get half a per cent of improvement to edge ahead of the competition, but there's nothing to encourage radical thinking and mad investment, stuff that really gets people talking.

For a while I thought about blowing a load of money on one of these properly historic bikes. I spent a while think-ing about buying a Britten when one was offered up for sale at £300,000. It was at the time I was buying the house I'm in now and I couldn't buy both. I made the right decision, 100 per cent, no regrets at all. Even at nearly half a million quid a go, they don't struggle to sell these Honda RC174 replicas. One came up for sale after I rode at Castle Combe and George Beale did contact me, but I never got back to him. I don't need bikes like these. It's someone else's mas-terpiece, not mine. I've realised if I've got spare money I'm better off ploughing it into my own shed to allow me to build my own stuff.

If I got the chance to ride the Honda again I'd snap their hands off. It was an amazing experience.

CHAPTER 7

'Loading shit in the trailer takes more precision than you'd think'

I'VE NEVER RELIED on racing or TV for money. Trucks were always Plan A, but the TV job means I could buy stuff like the pub or a tractor, to make sure I'm all right in the future. I bought my first tractor, a Fendt 9-Series, a few years ago so I could rent it out and earn a few quid while I was working on the trucks. For instance, the tatie firm pay £30 per hour and they pay for the diesel in my tractor. While I was at Moody's either my mate Tim Coles or his nephew young Ben Neave would drive my tractor. I'd get the rent for the tractor and they'd get the hourly rate for driving. On the days neither of them could do it I would.

Fendts are meant to be the Rolls-Royce of tractors, but mine was trouble so I sold it and bought a John Deere and it hasn't been a bother. It shouldn't be either, it's only a year and a half old. It's done 1,200 hours. That's how you rank a tractor. You don't say it's done 20,000 miles, you say how many hours it's worked. You might do 8,000 hours without anything major going wrong on a tractor like my John Deere.

A tractor like mine won't work from October to March, then it starts the muck-spreading, followed by the potato-drilling – that's planting the seeds. Tim does the shit-spreading, but loading shit in the trailer takes more precision than you'd think. There was a time when we had two tons of solid slurry in the bottom of the tank and that's what inspired a T-shirt we had made and sold on the Guy Martin Proper website. On the day the shit didn't hit the fan we were told we needed an agitator to stop the manure from solidifying. Nige the dog said he knew just the man, get Donald Trump on the job, the most effective agitator in the world.

The stuff in the trailer is called digestate. Round here a lot of it is unused and composted maize, wheat, barley, some pig shit from a big farm near here, duck shit from Cherry Valley in Caistor. Just general shit. You can use human waste as manure, but it has to be injected into the land, not spread. That's why I don't risk eating watermelons in places like India and China, because they sometimes use human shit on the land and the watermelons take it directly out of the soil.

The potato folk like the look of young Ben, so they're having him back to do the ridge-forming of the fields; that's another pass before the planting. I know what you're thinking: surely they'd run out of stones to collect by now, but in certain fields the stone always comes up through the crust. A farm near South Kelsey removed 300 ton of stone out of the land one year; when they went back to that same field four years later there was another 300 ton. It's real stony land in certain areas near me and it comes to the surface through ploughing. So, in the fields I work in they move the stones to the bottom of the ridges now. There's no point in removing them altogether, they reckon.

As I'm writing this there's a surplus of potatoes, because of a good harvest. When there is more supply than demand the price drops through the floor. In early 2018 the price of potatoes was £90 a ton, but they cost £160 per ton to grow. That's bad business, int it? But there are times when you can get £260 per ton. Potatoes don't seem to go in and out of fashion. Vegans eat them.

The John Deere had been sat there a couple of weeks, because most of the potato-drilling had been done. You need a big tractor like that to do the direct drilling work. Then we had Dot, so I was just doing a few bits from home.

At the back end of every summer, from August to October, the tatie-lifting job comes around. In 2017 things got dead busy, the tractor was in demand and Tim couldn't commit to it, so I told Moody I was doing the tractor job, twelve hours a day, seven days a week, for six weeks. In the end I stopped working at Moody's altogether. When Ben was in the tractor I was in the tatie-processing factory fixing plant or making guards for machinery. I was earning more money than I was at Moody's and it felt more constructive. There was no falling out, but it felt like it was time for me to move on.

The driving isn't hard work. It's just a case of following the tatie lifter. That's another tractor towing a trailer with usually four Lithuanian blokes sat either side of a conveyor belt, sorting the good potatoes from the bad. They have no idea who I am. They're kind of rude, but I like that. They don't have to be cheerful and they don't speak the language.

The blades of the tatie harvester go into the ground and pick the mud up and the potatoes buried in it. It has a big shovel, perhaps six-foot wide, that picks up three rows of potatoes at a time. It's all down to the driver about how deep the shovel goes. Too deep and you're picking up too much mud and the lads in the back have got too much to sort through; too shallow and you're cutting into your potatoes.

The driver has three or four cameras looking at different things: the shovel; the lads in the back; where he's going. It's a bloody busy job. I drive alongside, and the spuds that have been sorted are loaded onto my trailer. You have to be accurate, because the potatoes are being put in five-ton boxes. Some days I was doing 150 miles a day in the tractor, because you're back and forward to the depot to unload the potatoes. It was great.

An average day on the tatie job is get up at five, take the dogs for a half-hour walk, get back and have breakfast, fill my CamelBak and cycle ten miles to Elsham, where my tractor's parked when it's harvesting time and being used every day. I load two empty five-ton potato boxes and two one-ton boxes onto the trailer, then get on the CB to find out where the potato harvester is. It always leaves earlier than us. I leave the yard at seven. You might think it would be hard to find a field, out of all those in this area of Lincolnshire (there's no numbers on them), but we get told roughly where they are, then start looking for all the wheelings in the road, the mud and shit off the tractor tyres, as we get close. The company I work for has a road sweeper that clears up the worst of it after them, but you can still see the dust on the road. I've had days when I've needed a few detours to find the harvester, but I've never got lost.

Sometimes I'll sit for half an hour waiting for my turn in the queue, because there'll be two tractors doing my job, mine and one other. When one is full, it goes back to the factory to unload, and then I'll drive alongside the harvester. I have Radio 4 on. I like John Humphrys in the morning. I like how he has politicians stuttering. I like the stupid stuff on *Woman's Hour.* Then I change the radio over to Planet Rock. I have a book with me, or *Race Engine Technologies* magazine. I've been carrying my black book, a little notebook I'm always writing stuff in to help me remember good ideas and things to do. I started with it when I was building the Wall of Death bike.

I'll sit in the queue while they get the headlands done, the perimeter of the field, because it's bloody hard to run the harvester around the edge of the field and keep the tractor at the side of it, without squashing the taties, so they take their time doing that, then we're straight into it. I love it. It's another experience.

I nearly got stuck a couple of times, because when you're loaded up you've got up to 15 tons of potatoes on a big flatbed trailer, so pulling up a hill with that behind you is hard work. When you're moving about in a field and get slightly off-camber you think you're going to have the thing over, but it's always been all right. No one died.

There are times when I'll jump in the back of the trailer and pick through the muck for taties to help out. I'm there to work. If it's raining and the tractors can't get traction in the fields, they'll take the crew back to the factory and have them repairing the tatie boxes, because a fair bit of damage is done to them. The crew are over here and they're working. Fair play.

I can be out on a 12-hour shift, so I get back to the factory at about seven, then I'll fill the tractor with diesel, get all my stuff out of the cab and cycle home thinking how lucky I am.

Then, in November 2017, just after Dot was born, a local haulage company gave me a call saying that their two truck fitters were both off sick. They knew I was between jobs, so they asked if I'd give them a hand, see how it goes. I'd have enough stuff to do at home, but I like going to work, so I said yes.

They were understaffed because one of the fitters had steam-cleaned through his foot. I don't know how he did that, but it made a mess. His name is Mark Hooker, someone I've known for years, and the brother of my mate, Alf. Alf has to have one of the best names I've ever heard. Alf Hooker. Think about it . . . Mark had his boots on, but somehow this boiling hot jet from the steam cleaner had badly burned his foot. He carried on at work, but then his foot started swelling up in strange places, as if the water had got into it. From how it was described to me, it sounded a bit like a gunshot wound. It makes a little hole on the way in, but it's the mess it makes in the body and on its way back out again.

The other unfit fitter had had three lots of three weeks off and they don't know what's up with him. They showed me CCTV footage of him working on a wagon. He was on the top step, climbing into the cab, when he passed out and fell back and landed straight on his head. He didn't try to save himself or break his fall, it was just lights out. It must be a drop of summat like ten foot, from the height of his head on the top step to the ground. He's wasn't coming back for a bit.

The fleet operates for a cement company, so a lot of the work is on tankers that carry cement powder, ash powder, lime powder. They have 38 Scania trucks with 42 tanker trailers that need looking after too. I learned that the tankers have a blower system to pump the powder out. It channels into the bottom of a funnel. You need a massive blower on the truck to power it. The ones this fleet have are rated 1,500cfm, that means it can pump 1,500 cubic feet of air per minute. I have a fair size compressor in my shed at home, for powering pneumatic tools, and that's rated at 20cfm. The trailer's blower system runs off the truck engine, so I was having an interesting time learning all this.

The job got busy, so I was doing regular 70-hour weeks when there was no filming on. I wouldn't be getting home till ten some nights and I was up again at four. I love the pressure of it, making sure the job's done right and quickly.

I have sponsorship deals that pay decent money and the TV job pays well, and I've got so many projects at home that I'll tell you about soon that could keep me busy for the best part of six months. But none of this stops me wanting to get up at four or five in the morning to walk the dogs, have some porridge, get on my bike, ride to the truck yard, do 12 or more hours, then cycle home in the freezing cold and dark on shitty country lanes.

Do I need a psychiatrist? Friends think I do. Sharon certainly does. She thinks I'm mental. I don't know what it is. I'm addicted to it. By the time Saturday afternoon comes I'm knackered, good for nowt.

It can't be about the money, because I could earn loads more doing stuff for sponsors. You wouldn't believe the amount of paying jobs Spellman turns down that I've been offered. Money for doing not much, but I'm not interested. It has to be right. I'm not showing off, but if I asked Spellman to get me as many sponsors and as many paying nod, smile, agree days as he could I'd be rolling in money. But I don't. It's not part of some bigger business plan. I just don't want to do those things. I don't turn everything down; I'll do stuff with a company like Morris Lubricants, because they make good stuff that I use all the time, and they're an interesting company.

What I've realised is my priorities are not in sync with most other people's. Andy Spellman does a bloody good job, a job you wouldn't want, take it from me, organising

More sightseeing than going fast, in Bonneville.

First time on the dyno, getting it up and running.

Beer from the pub, more tea vicar.

Fish out of water, singing with Spellman at the pub.

Round Britain job,
beginning of the end …

Kawasaki H2R in the back
of the van, ready to race
but the rain came in.

Spain, Monteblanco. Fair swap.

Me and John McGuinness on the Mugens, on the first trip to Japan. What an honour and I'm the first person in history to crash one.

Asimo robot in Japan, Honda pushing the boundaries again.

Yamaha YZR in the Honda museum, Japan. Fair play to them for looking at other manufacturers for inspiration.

Honda NR500, Honda's most famous failure.

Prototype automatic motocross bike Honda CR250. Won in Japan and didn't do anything else.

Honda NR750, raced at Le Mans, amazing to see it and no tougher place to race it.

Bubba Shobert – legend.

Nicky Hayden's RCV211, size of the back brake disc – that's his flat track background.

Nine-speed gearbox, not often you see that.

Left below:
Honda's 50cc twin, four stroke.

Right below: Honda Six engine.

Composite NR500 built for the Japanese motor show in the 70s but it never left Japan.

Weston-super-Mare. Never had such a high heart rate for such a long period of time.

2017

PRI, the show of all shows.

this, that and the other for me and the businesses and contracts, woolly hats, the TV stuff, cleaning products,
sponsors and more besides. He'll spell things out and pri-
oritise them by how much he thinks I'll be into them and
what is realistic with the time I've got. 'Well, this is what it
is . . . this is what I think . . . could lead to that . . . pays you
that but you've got to do this . . .' Then it's down to me to
decide what I want to do. Quite often I won't give the idea
more than a few minutes' thought but the seed is there and
I'll maybe think about it another time, without committing
there and then. If I've said I'm preparing a truck for an
MOT, and put it in my diary, it doesn't matter what else it
clashes with, I'm doing the truck. I'm solid with that
whatever.

I say that I don't give a damn what people think of me,
but obviously I do, because it would break my heart if
people thought I was some media type. The most important thing is my opinion of myself. I don't ever want to look
at myself and think, you dickhead. I've done things in the
past and looked back at them and wondered, What were
you thinking? I suppose that's what being young is about,
doing things that make your older self shake his head.
Really I'm judging myself by my own standards. And when
it comes to those I'm quite set in my ways.

I do make things very difficult for myself. I'm the opposite of water. I never take, or even go looking for, the path
of least resistance. I'm wearing everything out, my brain,

my body, personal relationships . . . Why? I don't have an answer. Other than I want to break myself. Then what? I believe the body is a fantastic thing and it will repair itself and I'll go again.

It wasn't long ago that I was seeing a psychologist. In the run-up to the 2017 TT, after joining Honda, I contacted Prof. Steve Peters to see if he could tell me anything that might help me in racing. I've mentioned him in other books. He wrote *The Chimp Paradox*, a book a load of top athletes, especially Olympic gold-winning cyclists, recommended. I found it fascinating and it opened my eyes to the theory of the chimp, and how my chimp, Brian, was affecting my life, how I dealt with situations and how I could keep the chimp quiet. Many, if not most, people have an inner chimp that sticks their oar in. According to Peters there are three parts of the brain: chimp, human and computer. The chimp part gets the blood first, so it has the head start on making decisions and it isn't the most rational. It reacts, as the name suggests, in a territorial, animalistic way. I know my chimp was sometimes out of control, but because I had become aware of this I could, most of the time, count to three to let the rest of the brain assess the situation and get a grip on things.

There's a lot more to it than that, so I got in contact with Steve Peters, told him I was going back to race at the TT, and asked if he thought he could help me prepare.

All in all I bet we had seven or eight meetings. He doesn't know about motorcycle racing – it's not his world – so he'd quiz me about the races and I'd describe scenarios that could happen, or have happened, in a TT race. He'd go away, have a think about it, and the next time we met he'd say, 'Right, you need to do this in that situation. You need to have a prompt to put Brian back in his cage.' He explained that I couldn't just finish a lap and then refocus. Instead, before my mind has time to wander, there must be certain points of the track where I refocus. It doesn't matter what's happened; that's already happened, you're going forward, concentrate on what's going to happen, not what has happened. He was telling me to break it down into short, sharp sections. It's all about controlling the chimp, not allowing him to start questioning the job, to stop him asking, 'What are we fucking about with here?' Put the chimp in his box, to stop him from squealing. I learned that I've got fairly good control over the chimp, but I lose concentration and he was helping me with that.

Sometimes my life's a mess, because I've taken too much on, and I won't take days off from the trucks unless I really have to. That causes more grief, then I'll end up piling more on top. If I'm aiming for an end point, a goal, that is a dot on the horizon. I'll get there, but never by a direct line. It will happen; it's all the shit I have to deal with to get there.

Unfortunately it didn't matter how well I practised what Steve Peters taught me; it wouldn't make a shit's worth of difference on that bike, but it did help in other areas of my life. I look at my Ford pickup project, the one I want to build and race at Pikes Peak sometime in the future, and think, Right, I can get the gearbox on the engine and try that in . . . Then I realise, Hang on a minute, we've got two race bikes to build for the Neave twins (more on them later), the tractor needs servicing, the classic bike needs building . . . Which leads back to the question, Why am I working so much?

It might have been interesting to hear why Steve Peters thought I was so addicted to work, but, really, it's only worth finding out the reasons if I'm looking to get to the root of the problem so I can change. And, being blunt, I'm not. I'm happy how I am. The people around me aren't happy, and that's not a good situation, but I really can't see me changing much.

CHAPTER 8

'Ducking down to make sure I didn't bang my head on something that wasn't there'

LOADS OF IDEAS for new TV programmes get suggested, but not all of them fire me up. One, made in 2017, that had all the right stuff going for it was building a replica of a First World War tank to commemorate the 100th anniversary of the first successful use of tanks in battle. It had history, engineering, it was a massive undertaking and it had a very strong connection to Lincoln. I'm Lincolnshire, born and bred, but I was born in Grimsby, not Lincoln. It would have meant the same to me if the tank had been built in Gloucester or Sheffield or wherever. The important thing was to remind people what their city had created and to commemorate those who'd invented it, built it and fought in it.

The plan was to build a tank from scratch, then drive it through Lincoln city centre on Remembrance Day on that 100th anniversary.

Early on, we'd met with some of Lincoln council and explained what we wanted to do and why. We showed them how big the finished tank would be and we even had a length of rope that four of us, including two of the council staff, held into a rectangular shape that made the footprint of the tank, and walked up Lincoln's main shopping street to show how it would fit.

There isn't much left of the factory where those first tanks were built – it's now the Tritton Retail Park – but there's a statue commemorating the factory and its workers, and this Remembrance Day tank parade would be a respectful reminder of what the city and its workers achieved so long ago.

The tank was designed to try and break the stalemate of the First World War's trench warfare. Both the French and the Russians had designed great big contraptions, but neither had got past the prototype stage.

At that point in the war, Winston Churchill was the First Lord of the Admiralty, the political head of the Royal Navy, but he was also listening to the officers on the front line who were calling for an armoured vehicle. He formed the Landships Committee in February 1915 to come up with a plan for who should manufacture the vehicle the army so badly needed. The word was put out to companies with the relevant know-how (or so they hoped) to develop a fighting machine that, up until then, no one had thought of. In June the same year William Foster and Co. of Lincoln were given the contract to develop what would be called a tank. Fosters made agricultural machinery and road-going steam engines and they were the only company in Britain producing vehicles with tracks of the kind tanks would use. It was no bad thing that the winning company were based in Lincoln. For one thing, it was out of the way, so it was easier to keep secret.

One of Fosters' top men, William Tritton, and Major Walter Wilson came up with the design of the world's first tank and, in September 1915, Number 1 Lincoln Machine was shown to the powers that be. That first design was nicknamed Little Willie, the name the British tabloids gave to Kaiser Wilhelm II, the German leader.

Little Willie was flawed, but you had to start somewhere, and the next tank, Big Willie, was produced in February

1916. The official name was the Mark I. When it went into battle, in September 1916, it was clear the Mark I didn't have enough armour, but it scared the shit out of the Germans, so Fosters knew they were going in the right direction. Mark II and III followed, but never made it beyond testing. They got it right with the Mark IV and the government made an order for 1,000 tanks.

Because so many men were fighting, and dying, the First World War was the first time we'd seen large numbers of women employed in engineering. They were getting trained up and working, doing everything that needed doing, from welding to riveting, sometimes seven days a week.

The tank was invented to cross the no-man's-land between the front lines and break the deadlock between the German and British armies dug into trenches. Both were losing tens of thousands of men and not making any ground. The Mark IV first saw action at the Somme in 1916, then at Arras and Ypres the following year. Even though they'd been tested in England, they weren't prepared for the conditions of the Belgian and French battlefields and they got stuck in the mud. The tanks weren't the wonder weapon they were expected to be, not at first anyway. The army still had faith, though; they just had to find the right place to use them. That place turned out to be Cambrai in northern France.

I rode out to France to meet a local expert, Philippe Gorczynski, who had lived in the area all his life and now owns a hotel there. As a boy he used to go out in the fields and woods exploring and he'd find relics left over from the First World War – a bayonet, shells, all sorts of stuff – and he became fascinated with the battle.

We met at a war memorial for 7,048 officers and men who died at Cambrai. This wasn't the total number: it was far higher, over 80,000. These names were those of the bodies they couldn't find, the servicemen missing in action.

Philippe drove me out to where the British trenches ended and no-man's-land began, and explained how the tanks were used. The British had shipped 375 tanks across the Channel and driven them, during the night and at very slow speeds to keep the noise down, into position. The idea was to use the tanks to break the enemy's defensive position, the Hindenburg Line.

This defensive line was made up of thick rows of barbed wire, some above head height; then there was a gap, then more barbed wire and another gap. If anyone got to the barbed wire they would be shot at by German machine guns. If, somehow, they got past all that, they were into the Germans' three lines of heavily defended trenches.

At six in the morning, in late November 1917, the British lined up 375 tanks, followed by 6 infantry divisions, a total of 90,000 men, and all the available cavalry, 30,000 horses. As Philippe explained this, I could hardly believe it. Thirty thousand horses! And it was kept totally secret. How do you do that?

When the order was given, the tanks advanced. It wasn't just a wave of tanks; it was, as Philippe said, a tsunami, and, he went on to describe, 1,000 guns dropped a storm of steel on the Germans. Cambrai was chosen because it was land with good drainage, clay on top of chalk, and it wasn't all chewed up from previous battles, so the tanks stood half a chance of moving across it.

Before long, the Germans were panicking, and in two hours the line was broken. The tanks had gained more ground in twelve hours than the British had done in three months at other battlefields.

Nothing like it had been seen before, but within 24 hours 179 tanks were out of action, most of them broken down, with 60 damaged by enemy fire. This was a new plan of action, a new way of warfare, and the rest of the British forces weren't ready for it. The infantry and cavalry hadn't advanced behind the tanks and a lot of the ground they'd gained was recaptured by a German counter-attack. What no one was disagreeing about, however, was the success of the concept of tank warfare. It had been proven and it would be used again. There's no doubt the invention of the Mark IV shortened the war and saved many more lives because of that.

Philippe not only knew the area and the history of the Battle of Cambrai, he saved a major part of it. Years earlier an old woman, who was alive at the time of the battle, had told him that one of the tanks that had seen action in 1917 had been buried in the area and she knew where it was. It took six years to find it, but Philippe and his helpers dug it up and restored it as best they could.

The Mark IV tanks were either male or female. The males had two six-pounder cannons and two Lewis machine guns, while the females had five Lewis machine guns. The one they dug up was a female, called *Deborah*, the only tank to be left in the village of Flesquières. It's now stored in an old farm building. From one side it looks in good nick, but there's a hole where a shell has gone in. Walk round the back, though, and you can see the explosion has ripped the tank apart. The crew wouldn't have been much worse off in a bean can.

As part of the display there was a framed photo of *Deborah*'s tank commander, Second Lieutenant Frank Heap. As I was looking at the portrait of Heap, Philippe told me his grandson was staying in his hotel. It sounded like TV bullshit, but it was a total coincidence. Philippe rang the hotel and the grandson, Tim, a bloke in his late fifties or early sixties, came to meet up and tell us about his granddad.

Each of these first tanks needed a crew of eight to go into battle: driver; commander; four gunners and two gearsmen operating the gears for each track. You could say it was a bit cosy in there. When bullets hit the tank they wouldn't go through, but the crew would be showered with metal splinters coming off the inside of the tank's armour. They were given chainmail facemasks, but I don't know how many wore them. Conditions inside one of those early tanks were terrible, even without the enemy trying to kill you. There was heat coming off the engine and exhaust, the noise of the unsilenced engine sat in the middle of a metal hull right next to the crew, and then the serious threat of carbon monoxide poisoning from the fumes. No one had thought much about putting any kind of extractor fan in them, and they'd only do two miles to the gallon, so you can imagine the amount of fumes they were kicking out. It was so noisy in the tanks that the crew had to use simple sign language to communicate.

On the day *Deborah* was blown up, 23-year-old Second Lieutenant Heap and two of his crew climbed out to stretch their legs and see what was going on just as a shell hit *Deborah*, killing the other five crew. His grandson explained he lived to the age of 65, which was some kind of achievement considering how much he drank. He also said the family didn't know why the tank was called *Deborah*, because his wife was named Ruth.

Looking at this 100-year-old tank made me wonder what I'd have done in their position. The Mark IVs were dead unreliable and I love the challenge of keeping stuff working. The government would advertise in motorcycle newspapers for the right kind of blokes to crew them. I wouldn't want to be there, but I'd do what needed doing at the time, just like the millions who did just that in the 1914–18 war.

It was July when I visited France and met Philippe, and was filled in on all the background. We wanted to have a working replica made by November. The TV lot had found some great people and companies to try amd make it happen, but we were starting from scratch and only had six months, at best.

One lucky find was a 20-year-old German physicist, Thorsten Brand. He loved building models, but had found the ones he could buy weren't detailed enough for him, so he'd started making his own one-offs. His latest project was going to be a Mark IV. He'd been researching for years and had used old photos to make a near perfect 3D CAD solid model of a female Mark IV, the same as *Deborah*. By 'solid model' I mean a computer design, like industrial designers use. He was happy to share the CAD file, saving us a load of time. The TV lot had also got JCB on board, and they put one of their chief engineers, Martyn Molsom, in charge of their side of the job.

All Thorsten's data was fed into JCB's system and one of their young designers, Tom Beamish, spent weeks turning it into something JCB could manufacture within the time we had. Tom still had loads to do on the design side, because Thorsten had only drawn the exterior. When Tom was done I visited JCB's World Headquarters, at Rocester, Staffordshire. I was given a virtual reality headset and I could 'climb' into the tank Tom had finished drawing. I could open the doors, look down the gun barrels. I was crawling around on the carpet inside this virtual tank, ducking down to make sure I didn't bang my head on something that wasn't there. What a great system. It's the future.

Another important part of the team who made the tank a reality was Steve Machaye at Norfolk Tank Museum. He described himself as a self-taught mechanic, who started working on tractors at the age of 10 or 11, before moving into the military history side of things. He was massively excited when the TV lot contacted him. He admitted that he had thought, This isn't going to happen, but I like the sound of it so I'll talk to them. I can understand why he was sceptical. It was a massive, massive undertaking.

We visited his museum and Steve sketched out what had to be done in the simplest terms. He drew the sides of the tank, what he described as two rhomboids and what I called two oblongs on the slosh. Then he added the tracks.

He let me drive one of his collection, an ex-British Army Saladin Armoured Car. It is an 11-ton, 6-wheel-drive reconnaissance vehicle built in 1960. It does 45mph flat out, and about 30mph off-road. What a toy.

Other than Steve's knowledge, we needed him to supply a motor, gearbox and back axle. There are no original engines available for the Mark IV. The original one was a Daimler-Foster six-cylinder, German, and there was only one in existence. Going out in the Saladin was fun, but it was relevant too, because the motor Steve suggested for our tank was the same as in his six-wheeler. It's a Rolls-Royce B80 8-cylinder, 5.6-litre, water-cooled petrol engine that makes 160 horsepower.

The engine he was donating had never run. He'd owned it for 25 years and had bought it for £100. Damp had got to it over the years and it looked like it had been to the moon and back, but it was brand new, needed a check over and a lick of paint. We whipped the head off and saw it was all moving freely. Then Steve took us to a local agricultural salvage yard, where we found a suitable back axle, diff and gearbox still fitted to an old digger. This digger looked like it had been dumped there, years ago, to rot, but Steve got it going and I drove it around the yard to make sure the gears were all there. It was spot on. We'd bolt that to the Rolls-Royce engine back at the museum.

Back at JCB they were ready to start cutting and welding. The original tank panels were riveted together, but ours would be welded. To make it look like an original, JCB had made 3,000 rivet heads to weld to the body of the tank. The bottom of the hull of the original tank was made from a load of different plates, but our replica would be just two plates. No one would ever see under the tank, but it was still fitted with the right number of rivet heads. The attention to detail was impressive and the quality was something else. They were bending steel bar to an accuracy of +/- 1mm over an eight-metre length. Every piece of the puzzle was crucial, but the tank wouldn't have been built without JCB. What a brilliant company.

I spent most of the day with Chris Shenton, one of JCB's best welders, and he gave me a few pointers. His welding kit was a league above anything I'd ever used before. I wouldn't want their electricity bill.

Another company, Chasestead, a specialist prototype steelworking company, got involved to make the plates for the tank tracks. It was another bloody impressive place. They make equipment for the automotive and aerospace industries, top-secret stuff. They used a 4,000-watt laser to cut through the 12mm thick steel that the tank tracks were made from. It was cutting through it as quickly as you could draw the shape on a piece of paper. They made a load of the hatches, too. Our contact there, Justin Sedgwick, was dead impressed with the 100-year-old design and made it clear that even with their millions of pounds' worth of cutting-edge CNC kit it wasn't easy copying what the original engineers and factory had made. And back in the last century, Fosters of Lincoln went from making a few prototypes to producing summat like 1,000 tanks in six months.

To give the programme some relevance to the present day, the TV lot arranged for me to visit some of the current Royal Tank Regiment on Salisbury Plain. They were the same regiment that had been formed in 1916. A current tank commander, Lieutenant Winters, and a driver, Trooper Williams, showed me around the outside of the tank, telling me the Challenger 2 has the best armour of any tank in the world, but not even they know what it's made of that makes it so good. They reckon the British have never lost a

Challenger in action against the enemy. The cannon is accurate, deadly accurate, up to two kilometres. It's not a case of maybe hitting something: if it's within that two-kilometre range, it's going to hit it.

They handed me the black overalls, or coveralls as the commander called them, that only the Tank Regiment are allowed to wear. I could see from what he was wearing that there were loads of reminders of the Battle of Cambrai. The cap badge, worn on their berets, has a male Type IV on it, and the regimental colours are the same as flown on the flags that went into battle at Cambrai, the same brown, red and green I'd seen hung off the back of *Deborah*. Lieutenant Winters explained that the colours signified 'From mud, through blood to the green fields beyond'.

Even though the Challenger 2 hasn't been built since 2002, it's still current. I could climb into it, but the crew weren't allowed to film inside. The British Army has 52 of them and they cost £4 million each.

The Tank Regiment have 150 square miles of Ministry of Defence land to use on Salisbury Plain, and they took me out in a Challenger 2. It has 1,200 horsepower, so eight times more powerful than our 160 horsepower Rolls-Royce engine. It's got tracks, loads of metal and guns, but that's where the resemblance with the Mark IV ends. The new tank weighs 62 ton and will do 40mph. It needs only half the crew of the original tank, just four men, but it's more cramped than a Mark IV, because there is so much kit, gubbins, wires, boxes, guns, kettles, pissboxes . . . The ride was comfier than I expected. They can live in them for days.

They couldn't let me drive it, but I had my head out of the top while we were going full chat across the countryside. They were jumping the thing: sixty-two ton of tank, jumping! It would take off into these huge puddles, drenching everyone on board. It was covering ground a Land Rover would struggle with. It feels like it's shifting on the flat, but when it's going up hills it nearly peters out and starts cogging down the gears. You don't doubt the tank is going to get to the top of everything, but it knows about it.

To show some of what it could do they turned on the smoke generators, spraying neat diesel straight onto the exhaust and sending out a massive cloud of white smoke to act as a smokescreen. I was amazed how manoeuvrable these massive things are. They can do a neutral turn, spin 360 degrees on the spot. They don't like doing it, but they can do it when they need to. It was a brilliant day, another money-can't-buy experience to add to all the others I've had.

Back on our job, the main body of our tank had been finished and delivered to the Norfolk Tank Museum, in bare metal. It was an impressive thing. Steve was speechless when he saw it and painted the bare metal that night to stop it going rusty. Next time I went to see him we tried starting the engine, but it wasn't having it, so we spent the time fitting the track plates.

When I think back, not only was making the tank in less than six months a massive undertaking, there were so many other parts to this whole project. If I was going to drive a tank down Lincoln High Street, I needed to pass a test to prove I could be trusted with a tracked vehicle. A place called Total Driving was chosen to give me a lesson in a CVRT Stormer Shielder mine layer. It looks like a tank, with a flatbed on the back.

Another Steve was the instructor and he had me out on the road. I got the hang of it, but I did scare the shit out of the driver of a silver Transit van when I strayed into his lane. Steve had me parking, doing an emergency stop, the lot. This ex-army vehicle was dead responsive, but I went straight into the test feeling nervous. The driving part was all right, but I made a meal of answering the Highway Code questions. I still passed, though.

Everything was happening quickly, like it had to. Steve Machaye at the tank museum had investigated what was up with the engine and got it running a few days later, nearly blowing his hand off when it backfired through the carb. The next time we went to Norfolk, just a month before Remembrance Day, the engine and all the drivetrain was in the tank. Martyn, Chris and Tom from JCB came down to see the first test drive. We rigged up a piece of flat steel to operate as a temporary throttle. I was in charge of that and the clutch. Chris, JCB's welder, was the gearsman, and Steve was in charge of brakes that are used to steer the thing. The decision had been made to leave the top section of the hull off in case of fire, probably after seeing the mobile phone footage of Steve burning all the hair off the back of his hands.

We started it up and it sounded like a Lancaster bomber. Steve was nearly pulling levers out of the floor to allow him to turn. Going in a straight line was no bother. Everyone was all smiles. Then we tried to turn – and bang! The force of trying to steer the 30-ton tank caused one of the main drive sprocket bearing housings to smash. A catastrophic bearing failure is how we ended up describing it, but it didn't damage anything else.

JCB went back to the drawing board and designed and made a billet steel housing for the bearings, then welded mounting plates to hold it captive, right in situ in the tank. They did an amazing job. As soon as one problem was solved we had something else to deal with, but this was nothing some clever engineers would not be able to knuckle down to and get sorted. It was tight.

Parading the tank up Lincoln High Street on the 100th anniversary of the tank's first successful battle was always the plan, and I was looking forward to it, but it went pear-shaped. The police weren't happy and wouldn't let it happen. All the effort, all the significance of the place and the date, and it wasn't going to happen. Lincoln wasn't just number one on a list of possible places to do this: it was the *only* name we'd ever considered.

We were told the police said 11 November, Remembrance Day, is the busiest shopping day of the year and they couldn't risk having an untested vehicle driving through the pedestrian high street. Someone was obviously talking shit. All I could think was, You weak-kneed c***s. What that city did, in making the tank, and what it should have meant to them. Had they no respect? The whole idea was to show respect for those who had fought and died, and to show respect to Lincoln for the part it had played in the birth of the tank. I wasn't going to be at the helm and go mowing through Marks & Spencer or Costa fucking Coffee! When I heard their decision I was embarrassed to be British.

We needed a Plan B and that was to take the tank to the site of the battle, so on a wet 11 November we unloaded our replica Mark IV tank in the village of Beauchamp, near Cambrai. All the main folk involved in the programme and the making of the tank were there, from Thorsten the modeller, who'd spent four years researching and drawing it and could now see it in real life, to Martyn from JCB and Lieutenant Winters from the Royal Tank Regiment. By now the tank had been painted just like those that had fought at the Battle of Cambrai, and had been named *Deborah II*, in honour of the tank we'd visited.

With eight crew inside, picked from some of the loads of folk who'd helped make the tank, we drove up a country road towards the site of the front line. Steve, from the tank museum, had only done another ten yards' test drive in it since the bearing failure, so we were going into the unknown, but it worked a treat. All the rattling, clanking and engine revving was just like it would have been 100 years ago.

After the short drive we parked the tank and were joined by locals and some friends and family, before a bugler sounded 'The Last Post' and we had a minute's silence. Philippe, who was so passionate about everything to do with the tank and the battle, reckoned there couldn't have been a better place for *Deborah II* to make her proper maiden journey, but it was a shame we couldn't have done it in Lincoln, like we had planned and like so many people wanted.

The tank did go to Lincoln the following year. Steve from the Norfolk Tank Museum took it there, but they wouldn't let him start it, because of health and safety. If it wasn't for them who died for us we'd be leading a very different life to the one we lead now. I was still annoyed that they hadn't shown respect by allowing these things to happen.

The police got a lot of stick for their part in it, but came out saying it wasn't them who'd made the decision, that it was down to the council. I even had a word with the Freemasons but not even they could pull strings to get permission to drive a replica First World War tank up Lincoln High Street. What is the world coming to?

CHAPTER 9

'Married a Latvian former Nazi conscript; brought up five children, saw all those grandkids being born . . .'

OTHER THAN KATE, my youngest sister, who lives in the Lake District, the Martin family hasn't moved far from where we grew up. Sal is running the pub in Kirmington,

I'm a few miles away and Stu, my brother, is a few miles in the other direction. Since my dad retired, in April 2018, Stu has taken over the running of the truck business and changed the name to Martin Commercials. He has a couple of blokes working for him, including our cousin, Nick.

I don't see Stu often. I'm busy and he's living the job now, too, so he doesn't have much spare time either. I wasn't sure how he was going to do when he took over. He's been a retained firefighter for years, one of the part-timers who work other jobs, but do shifts on call and are paid for their time. If there aren't any calls they still get paid, but how busy they are, and how many calls they get, depends on the area they're in.

Back when I worked for my dad, which is going on for ten years ago now, I felt me and my dad would do anything to get the job done on time, working our bollocks off, but when my brother's beeper went off he'd clear off, however busy we were. Retained firefighters are dead important, I realise that, and he was doing a service to the local community, even saving lives, but I won't lie, it still did annoy me a bit.

I didn't work with Stu for that long, perhaps a couple of years, before my dad sacked me after I was pulled for having bald tyres on the works van I was driving. Stu's still a retained fireman now, but he has realised he can't run the truck business and be a firefighter, so he'll have to pack it in.

Stu asked our dad to ask me if I'd give him a hand in the yard, but I'm too busy and he'd have a job beating the place

I'm working. I enjoy it too much and have a good craic. I probably have a better time at work than I would if I was working on my own stuff full-time at home in the shed.

I didn't give Stu a straight answer, but knew I didn't want to do it. It's nothing to do with not wanting to take orders from my younger brother. I take orders where I am now. Perhaps I've learned not to mix family and work. It's different with Sal and the pub, because, as I've said, I have absolutely nothing to do with the running of the place. She does what she wants and makes all the decisions, never asking me for my opinion. That's how I wanted it. I wouldn't know where to start and that's why I say the Marrowbone and Cleaver is her pub. I don't want Stu going out of business and he won't do, because he's not shy of work. He doesn't need me.

When my dad retired part of me thought he'd be waiting to die, because he'd had so many years of graft, but it's the opposite. He's that busy he can't believe he had time to work. As well as helping with the maintenance side of the pub, he's tidying the church up, tidying the war memorial, making sure the bushes are cut. He wants Kirmo to be the best kept village in the area. Mum's still working three days a week as a nurse. She grew up in the same Caistor area, too, not ten minutes' drive from where me, Sharon and Dot live now.

Kate, who is the only one of my immediate family who doesn't live in North Lincolnshire, is definitely a Martin.

She used to be a race mechanic, now she's trained up to be a paramedic and she's a retained firefighter, too. She was called out to work on the fires on the Lancashire moors that made the news during the summer of 2018 when I was writing this book. She's got three young uns; she just gets on and does it. It shows it isn't just me who works.

I have written about my mum's mum, Granny Kidals, also known as Double-Decker Lil, and her late husband, my granddad Walter, in previous books. I used one of Walter's sayings for the title of the second book, *When You Dead, You Dead.*

Walter has been dead for a good few years and in January 2018 Lil passed away, too. She was 93 when she died. That is a bloody good innings and she had all her marbles right until the end. She fell over, at home, didn't even break anything, but she went into hospital, caught something while she was there, then got pneumonia and next thing she was dead. Pneumonia, the granny fucker, that's what they call it. It fucked my granny. She should have gone into hospital to get better, but shit happens.

Ninety-three years old! And she had a stroke when she was 40. She was probably the least fit of all my grandparents and she lasted the longest. I went to see her in hospital and she couldn't get about or owt, but she was on great form mentally. She still loved her gossip. Have you see this? Hurmmmm, what's your mother doing? That noise, Hurmmmm. It could be the start of a telling off or the beginning of her sharing some gossip. My mum makes that noise, too. She obviously got it from Lil.

My granny's house was a nice place, a bit tired, but nice, with about three acres behind it. I said I'd buy it, to keep it in the family, but one of her sons, my mum's brother, thought he could get more than it was valued for and put it on the market, but sales kept falling through at the eleventh hour. I wanted to buy it for the right reasons, but I'll leave them to it.

It was the house Lil and Walter had bought in the 1940s, when Walter had got the ferry over the Humber, from Hull, then cycled the 18 miles to see it.

The service for Lil was at Nettleton church, in the same village she'd lived in all her married life, and she was cremated at Grimsby Crematorium. It was a pretty small do and more of a celebration of life than a sad affair. If I can make it to anything like the same age I'll be over the moon.

It's good going the way Lil went, I reckon. Everyone's got to go, but I wouldn't want it dragging on for months or years. She was struggling to live by herself and she didn't want to go and live in a care home. She liked her independence. There was nothing sad about it, other than my mum has lost her mum. Lil had had a hell of an interesting life. She lived through the Second World War; married a Latvian former Nazi conscript; brought up five children, saw all those grandkids being born . . .

CHAPTER 10

'Hang on, boys. Who am I listening to?'

A WHILE AGO, Williams Grand Prix Engineering, that's the full name of the Oxfordshire-based Formula One team and constructor, got in touch with me through the TV lot. They wanted to know, 'Do you fancy helping restore a classic Formula One car, then racing it?'

When they first started talking about the job, I was going to race it in one round of the FIA Masters Historic Formula One series that allows drivers to race cars from the 1966 to 1985. It's an enthusiasts' series for what I'd describe as wealthy gentlemen drivers who want to keep driving the cars from what they reckon to be the golden age of F1. The website is proud to say the series 'takes us back to an era in which Cosworth DFV power and a creative car designer could win races, long before wind tunnels and energy drinks were created!' I don't know about the wind tunnel reference, because, in the motorbike world, Moto Guzzi were using wind tunnels to develop bikes in the 1950s and 1960s, so I'm sure Formula One designers were experimenting, too.

The Masters series doesn't allow drivers to race 'ground-effect' cars, the ones with massive side pods and little skirts between the side pods and the tarmac. They're designed to make the car pull itself to the floor, giving it massive downforce and grip, all to increase corner speed. F1 cars have had front and rear wings to create downforce, before and since the ground-effect era, but wings and spoilers are not the same. Ground effect is when negative pressure is created under the car, by using the track surface itself as part of the car's aerodynamics. By reducing the air pressure below the car it increases the grip without the drag of big wings and spoilers. Designers used all different methods to create ground effect, including great big fans that sucked the air from beneath the car to lower the pressure.

Formula One banned ground effect for the 1983 season, and the car I was going to drive was from the first season of the post-ground-effect era, but other series still experimented with the theory. Developing racing car aerodynamics can be a dangerous game. Le Mans prototypes, that look like road-going supercars, not open-wheel F1 cars, want to improve their corner speed too, but when they've got their aerodynamics wrong, like Mercedes did in 1999, it goes pear-shaped in a dramatic way. That year's 5.7-litre V8 Mercedes Le Mans prototypes, that were raced by Mark Webber and Peter Dumbreck, took off at 190mph and flew 15 or 20 feet in the air, before flipping and landing back on the track. Porsche have had the same problems in Le Mans series races, too

The car at the middle of the TV programme was the Williams FW08C. It's powered by a Cosworth DFV, 3.0-litre V8, the most successful F1 engine ever. It won everything from 1969 up to 1982. Before 1969 you could race all sorts, but it was linked to weight limits, so the bigger the engine, the heavier the car had to be. At different points in F1's history you could have supercharged engines, 18 cylinders, V12s, all sorts of rare stuff, all out together.

F1 rules have changed over the years, sometimes to reduce costs, other times to increase speeds, especially when sportscar racing classes were getting more attention than Formula One cars. In 1966, when the FIA increased the engine size from 1500cc, they decided on 3.0-litre naturally aspirated (that means it has carbs or fuel injection) or engines with half the cylinder capacity but with forced induction – so turbos or superchargers. There were weight limits, too.

The Cosworth DFV didn't win overall in its first year of the new rules. It suffered from cam drive gear failures, but as soon as the teething problems were solved it went on to win over 150 F1 races in different constructors' chassis.

The founder of Williams, Frank Williams, became a team owner in 1969, three years after he started Frank Williams Racing Cars. The current company, Williams Grand Prix Engineering, started out as a team in 1977, using someone else's chassis. They only did that for a year, swapping the March chassis they'd bought for one of their own. Their first chassis was designed by Patrick Head, one of the most famous names in F1 technology, and co-founder of the company with Williams.

When it came to the TV programme, the goalposts had moved and it turned out I wouldn't be racing in the Historic Formula One series, because I didn't have the right level of car racing licence; it would have taken a load of races to get it, and Williams weren't keen on the FW08C being in that kind of race. So now they were trying to have me do some driving challenge against Jenson Button, who, everyone hoped, would be in another 1980s Williams F1 car. I'd got to try beat him, but it would be a handicap race, because Jenson was a former F1 world champion. I was a bit disappointed it wasn't a proper race, but I still had the chance to drive a Formula One car, which was something special – even if it wasn't the first time.

When I went to Monteblanco in March 2017 to do my first test with the official Honda team, I got there early and saw there was a classic Formula One team testing. I had a look in the garage where the classic race car was parked and one of the blokes, who turned out to be the team owner and driver, said, 'What are you going here?' I told him I was going to ride the Honda. He knew about my Pikes Peak bike and I told him I had it in the van. 'Bloody hell,' he said, 'does it go?' 'Course it does,' I replied. He said, 'Let me have a go on that and I'll let you have a go in my Formula One car.' I said, 'You'll do for me.' I couldn't believe it.

It was a proper Formula One car, and I had five laps in it. It was brilliant. The owner didn't give me any special instructions. He just said, 'You might need first gear, but I don't think so. Be a bit careful around the hairpin.' I'd never seen the track before and I was going out in a full 1980s Formula One car. Big back wing, full aero, Cosworth DFV, trick as . . .

He rode my Martek in his race overalls and he wasn't hanging around. Brave man. Wearing those he'd be all right if he set on fire, but not if he ended up sliding down the track. So if the TV lot say it's the first time I've driven an F1 car, you know the truth . . .

One of the reasons the car we're restoring is so valuable is because Ayrton Senna took his first ever F1 test, at Donington Park, in 1983. If you look at the statistics and count the wins, Senna doesn't stand out. He had three world titles, in 1988, 1990 and 1991, compared to Michael Schumacher's seven, and he didn't have a personality like Valentino Rossi, but he's seen as one of the all-time greats by F1 fans, and was even when he was driving, because his skill level was a league above anyone else he was driving against. He held the record for pole positions, but he wasn't always in the best car, especially when the Renault Williams was dominating.

Senna had a real good test in the FW08C we were making the programme about. He was fast – faster than Williams's regular driver, Keke Rosberg, who was the reigning F1 world champion – but the Williams team didn't have any openings for the young Brazilian, so Senna joined Toleman for the 1984 season.

It doesn't only have the Senna history: Keke Rosberg won the 1983 Monte Carlo Grand Prix in it, too.

The FW08C has a tubular, semi-monocoque chassis. The DFV engine – that stands for double four-valve, because it was based on an existing four-cylinder Cosworth engine, with four valves per cylinder – was the first to be used as a stressed member in F1 racing. The gearbox is bolted to the back of the engine, and the tub, the part of the car the driver sits in, is mounted to the front of the engine. An engine that acts as a stressed member forms part of the chassis of the car and the suspension is mounted off the back of the gearbox. It predates the use of carbon fibre, so the bodywork is alloy sheet. The wishbones are TiG-welded steel: beautiful things. It's been sat in the Williams museum for years and if I was going to drive it, hopefully hard, everything needed a proper going through.

Every original component had to go through a process of NDT, non-destructive testing, whether it's dye-penetrant or magnetic particle inspection. With the first of those processes you dye the part and if it has any cracks that aren't normally visible, the dye shows them up. There are other methods that use magnetic particle powder that highlights the cracks in a part that can take a magnetic field, so not aluminium or its alloys.

The first day of filming was in January 2018, at Williams in Wantage, Oxfordshire. I was shown around the car by Jonathan Williams, Frank's son. He runs the heritage side of the company and knows the history of every car, including the FW08C we were involved with. Williams Heritage has the largest collection of F1 cars in the world, with more than 120 cars.

Two days later I was at Bruntingthorpe, the test track in Leicestershire, to meet a test driver, a bloke called Rob

Wilson. Eleven of 2017's Formula One drivers had all been trained by him.

While we were waiting for Rob I was getting to know Karun Chandhok, who was going to be one of the experts involved in the TV show. He's Indian, about the same age as me, with loads of racing experience and a bit in Formula One, but only a bit. He's one of F1's TV pundits, too. He told me that Rob Wilson wouldn't be what I was expecting and that he'd teach me to get my eye in on the test track. I think Karun has missed his chance to be a full-time F1 driver, but he does drive the current cars as one of Williams's test drivers. Williams Heritage had just rebuilt the FW14B, the car Nigel Mansell won in, and he tested that.

Rob Wilson rocked up in the car he was going to teach me in, some Vauxhall diesel rental. He's 65, smokes 60 a day, from New Zealand originally, but has lived over here for 50 years, plays bass guitar in a country band called Grand Prairie. A right normal bloke, a good shit wouldn't hurt him, but he's faster than all the F1 drivers, if they were all driving his dead normal hire car. He explained that there's nothing better than a bog stock car for understanding the benefits of the methods he teaches.

I don't profess to be any kind of driver, so Williams wanted Rob Wilson to tell them if he thought I was up to driving the historic F1 car. They wanted to be sure I've got a feel for it. I got 100,000 miles out of the brake pads in my Transit, so course I've got a feel for it, but they wanted their man to tell them. Some drivers are with him half a day, others are with him 20 days a year. Williams are sending drivers to him and they wouldn't trust me unless he gave me the all-clear.

First of all I got in with him while he drove for a few laps. 'It's all about getting the car in a steady state,' he said. He kept saying you want a flat car, you want it going in a straight line, because every time you're putting any steering input in, it's sapping power from the car. You should always make everything as straight as possible so, don't drag out the turns. Make them short and sharp, to get it going in a straight line again. This was the opposite to how I thought it would be. I'd try to be smooth and flowing, but that's not the key. Instead, brake really late, really hard, then turn sharp, instead of making a nice sweeping curve through the corner. Do this and you make a hairpin into a diamond.

There are marks on the runway that he puts cones on to mark out a course. It's a course he's used for years and some of the corners simulate corners on famous racetracks. There's a mixture of tight stuff and fast stuff.

Every now and then he'd say, 'The brakes need to cool down', but what that meant was he needed a fag. He was a good professional racer. He raced in America, in Indy cars, but he stopped racing professionally when they put a smoking ban on flights.

When it's my turn we put our seatbelts on, but we're not wearing helmets. I have Rob in the passenger seat and Karun in the back.

We get going and they were both shouting at me, so I ended up spinning the car a couple of times. I was getting all this information, and ended up having to say, 'Hang on, boys. Who am I listening to? Tell me what you want me to do and let me get on with it. Stop barking at me while I'm trying to do it.'

After a couple of sessions I got my eye in, then it started raining. We had another couple of sessions, then it really started pissing it down, so we couldn't do any more. I was definitely quicker at the end of the day, and Rob told Williams I'd be all right.

Two weeks later, in early February, I was at Pembrey, in South Wales, having my first proper drive in a single-seater, because Monteblanco was just messing about. This time I was in a Formula Three car. You have Formula One, the GP2, then Formula Three. Both Sebastian Vettel and Lewis Hamilton came through Formula Three.

The car I was driving was powered by a 2.0-litre, normally aspirated, four-cylinder Mercedes engine and had an Italian Dallara chassis. I was with Karun again. First he showed me round in a hire car. It was pissing it down again, and this time it didn't stop all day. After that, Karun was in another F3 car and if it had been dry I would have tucked in closely behind him to follow his lines and learn where he was braking, but because of the wet track I wouldn't be able to see anything for the spray, so I had to go out and drive the single-seater on my own. When I came back in the pits, we'd look at the telemetry and he'd say, 'You can do that here and you can do this there.'

I couldn't believe the downforce and grip from this car. It was really impressive. Pembrey isn't a long track, but I was 1.1 seconds a lap off Karun's time. The car he was in had a paddle-shift, little levers attached behind the steering wheel that you pull with two fingers without taking your hands off the wheel, but mine had a regular gear lever, because the old Williams would have a gear lever and they wanted me to get used to that.

Another two weeks later, in mid-February, I caught up with some of the restoration at Judd Power, the company restoring the car's Cosworth DFV engine. John Judd founded the company in 1971. He worked for the racing driver Sir Jack Brabham, spannering for him, and Judd and Brabham started the company together. Now it's a company of 25 people, and they've worked with Lotus, Honda, Yamaha, Mazda, Toyota and Nissan. They used to build Formula One engines. In the 1980s and 1990s, loads of teams, including Lotus, Tyrrell and Arrows, used Judd engines, and Williams got a couple of podiums with them when Nigel Mansell was driving for them. They've developed LMP1 and LMP2 Endurance racing engines, too.

Judd were given the job of rebuilding the engine for this car. Williams have always just been chassis specialists, a constructor in F1 jargon, who worked with engine manufacturers like Cosworth, Honda, Renault and Mercedes.

Dan, a young bloke who works for Judd, stripped the engine in October 2017 and it took nearly four months to check everything, to make sure there weren't any weaknesses. The Cosworth has lightweight magnesium engine cases and they can deteriorate over time. If it chucked a con-rod it would wreck the whole engine. It turned out pretty much everything was in good nick, but they didn't know that. I helped put the top end on and set the timing, working with Dan. It was interesting.

Judd Power have a good reputation and some real oddball stuff is brought to them. They had a V12 Ferrari with radial valves in the cylinder heads when I visited.

With a programme like this I'm spending a day here and a day there while things are happening, then going back to work in between. But as far as filming for this went, everything was put on hold because I was being sent to Russia for three and a half weeks.

CHAPTER 11

'It was me who came up with the idea of Russia'

Посольство России

IT WAS THE back end of March 2018 when I had to drive to London to get a Russian work visa for a big filming job we were doing out there. I wasn't mad about going to London. I never really am. As usual, I'd been flat out at work, and I was supposed to have gone to Manchester to sort the visa out, but that didn't happen for some reason to do with the Russian Embassy.

If March 2018 doesn't ring any bells, it was the same month the former Russian military intelligence officer Sergei Skripal and his daughter Yulia were poisoned by the nerve agent Novichok in Salisbury. From what I've heard and read, it sounds like Skripal had been a double agent in the 1990s and when the Russians found out, in 2006, they sentenced him to 13 years for high treason. He didn't get close to serving all that because he was traded in a spy swap with the West in 2010. His daughter was visiting him from Russia when they were poisoned. Everything pointed to the Russian government ordering the poisoning, and it didn't take long for the shit to hit the fan. The Prime Minister Theresa May didn't take kindly to the thought of the Russian government attempting to murder a foreign spy in Wiltshire and started expelling Russian diplomats, like governments used to during the Cold War years.

All this would have been interesting enough, but we were supposed to be flying out to Russia for three weeks of filming on 21 March, just over two weeks after the poisoning.

The day before going to the Russian Embassy I'd been on a CPC (Certificate of Professional Competence) course in Yorkshire. I've had a truck licence since 2009, and I've taken trucks on MOTs, but I'm not allowed to drive a truck with a paying load in it without a CPC. You can drive a farm tractor on the road with a 40-ton load on a provisional licence, but if you're a truck driver you've got to do 35 hours of classroom-based lessons over the space of five years. I've never done it, so I've got to do the training before they let me drive. There was no need to have this training when I was at Moody's because I was only delivering the tractor units or trucks with an empty trailer. At the new place I'm working I have to take trucks for MOTs with a load on, so they can test them with the correct axle weight.

Anyway, I got home from that and heard the news that it was either the Kremlin that had ordered the attack, or the Russians had lost control of the nerve agent and it got into someone else's hands to be used. Theresa May said if she didn't get an answer within 24 hours, things were going to get serious. It sounded like she half meant business. The 24 hours she was waiting for an answer in was the same 24 hours I had an appointment to get my visa.

I went through the process of going to London because I didn't want to get to the eleventh hour and think, Shit, it is happening, and not have the paperwork sorted. Still, at the time I was driving down the A1 I was pretty sure the Russia trip wasn't happening. I didn't doubt we'd get a visa, but when we landed in Russia would they turn us, a British television film crew, around and send us back on the first flight out?

I read the book *Red Notice* by Bill Browder, an American businessman who is now a British citizen, a few years ago and it gave me a different view of Russia. In the 1990s, as

Russia ditched Communism to become the capitalist dictatorship that it is today, the government gave shares of the nationalised utilities and services, like gas, the bus service, train service and telecoms, to the masses in the form of tokens. The oligarchs got millions' worth, but every adult in Russia owned a fraction of a percentage of Gazprom, or whatever. Browder ran his own investment company, moved to Russia, got half wise to this, started buying these tokens from Russians, and over the years he ended up owning 51 per cent of Gazprom or summat. It was legal, but the Russian powers that be didn't like it so they made life very difficult for him and in 2005 deported him. The Red Notice of the book's title is the Interpol extradition request the Russians put on Browder to bring him back to Moscow to stand trial for fraud and tax evasion. The court case went ahead without Browder and he was given a sentence of nine years, to be served if they ever get hold of him. So Browder knew all about this side of Russia and how it all worked, when he heard about a lawyer, a young bloke called Sergei Magnitsky. The lawyer discovered that Russian officials were involved in a fraud of $230 million. When he wouldn't back down and keep quiet, the officials pulled strings for Magnitsky to be put in prison. According to *Red Notice*, Magnitsky was tortured over months before being beaten to death by eight secret police.

This all adds to my fascination with Russia. No one's ever beaten the Russians at their own game. I really enjoy making the travel programmes. We've done Latvia, India and China and it was me who came up with the idea of Russia when Channel 4 said they wanted more of them. Because it's such a big place, with so many interesting stories, the time away was a lot longer than I hoped it would be. It was supposed to be three weeks, then somehow it grew to four, but then back to three weeks and three days. I'd prefer three weeks or less, but there was no way to fit in everything the director wanted to film, so that was that.

We had a fair-sized crew ready to head out to Moscow and we all had our visas, but the flights still hadn't even been booked and we were due to leave in less than a week. I didn't know the plan of what we were going to do out there. I knew we were going to Siberia and Chernobyl, but I never ask. I just go for a look and take it as it comes. If they let us in.

CHAPTER 12

'Terminal 4, that said a lot. Usually you only fly to wanky places from Terminal 4'

IN BETWEEN BEING given our work visas and the day we were supposed to be flying to Moscow there had been plenty of talk between North One and Channel 4 about if we were going to get into Russia or not. North One are the production company. They make programmes for Channel 4, BT, Sky, the BBC or whoever. Nearly all my programmes have been made for Channel 4, but North One are independent; they work for whoever wants the programme idea they're coming up with. It just so happens that Channel 4 wants the kind of stuff they make with me.

North One told Channel 4 that they didn't want to risk sending us out, paying for all that travel, just for us to be sent home on the next plane. We all felt it was touch and go. North One's top bods were talking to Channel 4, who had commissioned the programmes, explaining that they felt nervous about the whole job. From what I picked up, it sounded like North One were all ready for selecting reverse and they put the decision in Channel 4's hands.

Channel 4 did their research and told North One to risk it, buy the tickets, book the hotels and if it all went wrong they'd cover it so that North One were not out of pocket. So that was it. Only a few days before we were due to fly, it was decided we really were going, but I still didn't know how long we would be in Russia before we were deported.

I'd told them, 'Well this isn't happening, is it?' James, the director who'd be working on all the Russia stuff, said the same. We'll get to Heathrow and get turned away. Or we'll get to Moscow and get turned away, or we'll start filming on day one and be deported. That's how we felt it would be as the ten of us met at Heathrow Terminal 4. Terminal 4, that said a lot. When was the last time you flew from Terminal 4? Usually you only fly to wanky places from Terminal 4.

Most of the crew were people I've worked with for years. James, the director, he runs the show really. Nat and Max, the cameramen, and Andy, the soundman. There was Amy and Jess, the producer and assistant producer, who do loads of jobs between them, logging the filming details, noting everything for future reference, sorting it all out on the day, dealing with the paperwork, keeping everyone happy and running as smoothly as possible. Then there was Aldo and Stu. Stu is the medic and Aldo is the minder, the security. They're both ex-Royal Marines.

The only person I hadn't worked with before was Matt, another soundman, but he turned out to be shit hot, too.

The ructions caused by the Salisbury nerve agent poisoning were still the main news on every radio station. They weren't talking about much else. Twenty-three Russian diplomats had been kicked out of Britain, and 20 other countries expelled a load of other Russian diplomats in solidarity with the British government. The Kremlin wasn't happy.

We were booked on a morning flight, four hours straight to Moscow. I was so sure I was going to be back in London that night, I was already making plans. I'd promised myself that I wouldn't go back to work, but I'd use the time I was supposed to be away working on my classic race bike, getting the Ford P1000 pickup project started. I'd get this done, get that done: I was looking forward to getting caught up.

The first thing that made me think I was right, and, yes, we would be sent back, was seeing four UK Border Force guards stood at the entrance to the bridge to the plane as we handed our passes in to board. I'd never seen that before.

We landed in Moscow, showed our passports and walked straight through. We were all nervously looking at each, trying to play it cool, but we didn't need to because the passport control officer didn't bat an eyelid at us. We had to wait, as normal, about half an hour for the 30 extra bags that a camera crew travel with, and have all the carnets certified. The carnets are the temporary import licences for all their kit, so they don't have to pay import tax on them. There were no problems there either.

In the arrivals hall we met Mikhail Smetnik, the fixer. He told us to call him Misha. I'd say he was in his late fifties, early sixties and dressed like you'd imagine a professional 60-year-old Muscovite would. He blended in, like a typical grey Russian who wants to go about his business. In all the years we've done these things, he was probably the most efficient fixer we've ever had. He was on the money. All the other places we've been we've used a couple of fixers, but not this time. Misha knew everyone.

A fixer lines up all the jobs. If we want to film on the Moscow Metro, the underground train system, you can't just walk in and start filming; it's the fixer's job to organise all the permits in advance. Not an easy job, especially in Russia. Misha was a really knowledgeable bloke, spoke very good English, was really clever, witty, understood the British sense of humour. He stayed with us for the whole job in Russia.

Almost as soon as we met Misha we were asking how things were looking and he said it was all pretty good. There were a couple of things he had problems with – getting a flight in a MiG fighter jet was looking doubtful, because of the military associations and the whole diplomatic situation was affecting that – but everything else seemed business as normal.

Looking out of the window as we drove into the middle of the city, Moscow felt very Western, industrial, with snow piled up 20 feet high at the side of the roads and very square buildings. It was minus four or five degrees when we landed, nothing too stupid. I was warm enough in my truck driver's trousers with the reflective strips around the bottom, John Deere coat and Five Ten shoes. I was still wondering when we were going to get turned away.

We stayed at a Marriott right in the middle of Moscow. The hotel could have been anywhere in the world. That was the first of four nights in the Russian capital, before we flew to another town. Looking out of the window I'd see a constant flow of people, going to and from work. It didn't feel like England, but it didn't feel as foreign as, say, Japan.

It felt like Russia. I liked the fact that I couldn't recognise any of the words on signs, because they're all written in the Cyrillic alphabet. A lot of women would be dressed in big coats, but short skirts. Russians like their short skirts, even in the middle of winter.

The next morning we got straight into the filming, and all 11 of us first travelled in two people carriers to Red Square, arriving there at ten. I could see Lenin's Tomb, with the Kremlin, a collection of buildings that includes President Putin's official residence, and St Basil's Cathedral in the background, with its famous brightly coloured domes. The camera turns on and James, the director, asks, 'What are you thinking?' I say summat like, 'Well, we're here.' I was still dead surprised. This was it. We were filming in Russia, and the idea of that took a little bit of getting used to.

I talked to James, while I was being filmed, like I'd talk to any of you. I explained that we're getting all this gobble-degook back home, propaganda, if you want to call it that, Theresa May is saying we aren't taking it lightly. The nerve agent that was used on the Skripals was Russian. Boris Johnson is giving it all the spiel about Porton Down, where the Ministry of Defence has their Science and Technology Lab, who have confirmed there's no doubt the poison was Russian and that the British government is sending diplomats back to Russia. It sounded serious, and I honestly thought we wouldn't get to film, but there we were, right at the heart of the beast. You can't get more Russian than Red

Square. When soldiers appeared and asked for our permits to film, Misha sorted all that out.

I looked around and could see what I was sure were FSB men. The FSB, the Federal Security Service, are the secret service that took over from the KGB. They all wore earpieces, the grey men, in the background, watching. They also came up and said something to Misha, who gave them the right paperwork, and it was a case of, OK, go about your day.

After all that worry about being sent home, turns out Russia really do not give a fuck about Britain or what we do. We're insignificant. It's like the Isle of Anglesey declaring war on England. All right, mate, what are you going to do about it? That's what we are like to Russia.

The Russians have got a history of this, so I didn't have any doubt it was them that tried to kill the double agent, but, in a way, I think that's good. You know not to fuck with them. Fuck about with England and what do you get? At the worst a strongly worded letter or six months in a well-furnished prison cell?

By now we realised that we were back to Plan A: make a telly programme and fly home in three and a half weeks. Now it was a relief to get started filming. It had been my idea to go to Russia in the first place, thanks to my fascination with the place, so we were only doing what I'd asked.

Across Red Square I could see people queuing in minus five to see Lenin's Tomb. The leader of the Bolshevik Revolution, that overthrew the tsars and turned Russia Marxist, and the first leader of the Communist Soviet Union, Lenin was a doer and his body has been on show, except for during the Second World War when they hid him somewhere else, since he died in 1924. And still folk are queuing up to see him.

Stalin used to be on show there, too, until the Communist Party started to distance themselves from him. You could say Stalin ran a tight ship. Under his leadership the USSR sent nearly two million people to the gulags, the brutal labour camps folk who weren't in line were sent to; many of them were political prisoners, some were teachers and lecturers, basically anyone Stalin didn't like the look of. Of those two million he ordered the execution of over 600,000. After Stalin died in 1953, Nikita Khrushchev came to power and started letting some people out of the gulags, and slightly improving conditions. They didn't exactly turn into holiday camps, but he'd let the prisoners get clothes and letters sent from their relatives. Khrushchev's thinking was he didn't want the Communist Party linked with Stalin and the abuses of the people, and what he called 'the cult of personality' that allowed Stalin to get away with what he did when he ruled the country by fear. Again, Russia hardly transformed itself into Butlins under Khrushchev, but it was nowhere near as bad. They call what Khrushchev started the process of de-Stalinisation. So Lenin stayed in the tomb, but Stalin was moved out of the Kremlin to a spot in the Kremlin Wall Necropolis.

We were in Red Square for a couple of hours, watched the changing of the guards, then went to the Federation Towers, two skyscrapers, one 97 storeys tall, the other 63, to meet a bloke called Kirill Vselensky. In his late twenties, he is what's known as a rooftopper. His hobby is climbing the highest buildings he can find, anywhere in Russia; when he reaches the highest, most awkward bit, he takes a photo of himself. He's not the only one who does it; it's a thing in Russia. We met on the top of the roof, but I didn't do anything daft.

He looked like just a normal bloke; you wouldn't have any idea he did such extreme, hardcore stuff. He spoke a bit of English, much more than my Russian, which still doesn't extend much further than hello, so we spoke through a translator.

He had an iPad and showed me some of the hardcore rooftopping he'd done in Vladivostok, on the tops of bridges, also without any safety equipment or harnesses. I quizzed him, asking if he was just doing it for Facebook followers, but he wasn't; he likes doing it and does it for the buzz, taking pictures to show where he's been. I could see the similarities between him rooftopping and me road racing. The fact that it could kill us both was part of what made us want to do it. In his game, you have to be concentrating or it's curtains. You can get fairly well arrested for it, too.

Kirill told us he used to live in a flat with his mate, who was also a rooftopper. You can get away with a lot of it; you might get a small fine for trespassing, as long as you don't do anything political. Try anything that the authorities think is provocative and they are after you. Kirill's flatmate climbed up somewhere and painted a Ukrainian flag over the Russian hammer and sickle. There are big divisions in Ukraine between those who want the Russians to have more of a hand in running the country and those who want it to stay totally independent, and it led to a crisis when Russia annexed Crimea, placed in the Black Sea off the coast of Ukraine, in 2014. There'd been trouble in Ukraine in 2004 when an opposition leader and presidential candidate, Viktor Yushchenko, was poisoned, but survived. So, the Russian secret service is touchy about anything Ukrainian.

After Kirill's flatmate posted footage of himself online rooftopping and painting the blue and yellow flag of Ukraine over the Russian hammer and sickle, the FSB came around to their flat, but only Kirill was in. He hadn't been political and said he wasn't involved in the incident, but the FSB were after anyone they could make an example of, so they searched the flat, found some drugs and locked him up for a year and a half. He didn't want to talk about it; you can only imagine what it must be like in a Russian prison for a young bloke who'd been fitted up.

I also met another rooftopper, called Angela Nikolau. We met in SIXTY bar on the 62nd floor of the poshest skyscraper in Moscow. She won't have been 25, and got a load of modelling contracts out of doing what she does and sharing it on social media. She's been used for laptop and phone adverts and travel companies have sent her and her boyfriend – who is also a roofer, as they also call them – around the world to climb buildings and make films and photos for them. Again, like Kirill, I thought she was doing it all for Twitter followers and all that, but she loved it. She says she was going to stop rooftopping so often, but she still loved the buzz of it. When her grandparents see photos of her on the top of buildings, she tells them they're fake, that the pictures have been Photoshopped, so they don't worry about her.

When you're on a job like this, away from home, the crew are together for the whole time, meeting early in the morning, working together all day and eating together at the end of the day. Except for a couple of people who are full-time for North One, the rest are freelancers who get booked when there's work. I don't know if that's the reason, but there can be an exponential ball of arse-kissing when all the crew eat together at the end of the day and I don't like that, so sometimes I go off and do my own thing. I tell them, I don't just disappear, but I leave the hotel and find somewhere to eat on my own. They're all good lads and lasses, but I need to get out on my own for a bit. I never got too far from the Moscow hotel, but I would go for a walk, a few roubles in my pocket; spot a restaurant somewhere, a bit oddball if possible; point to something on the menu and have a cup of tea or a beer. The tea was good,

Russian caravan tea. I love people-watching, and that's easier when you're on your own. I love that no one knows who I am, no one gives a fuck who I am. I can just watch the world go by. There are nights I eat with the crew, but not every night. It's healthy to have a bit of your own time. Everyone needs that.

The next day we went to Star City, the Yuri Gagarin Cosmonaut Training Centre and the Russian space museum where we were shown around by a young bloke called Dimitry. He was only in his early twenties, but what a clever bloke.

I'm fascinated by the Russian space race. I love the story of how much the Americans spent on developing a pen that would work in space, and the Russians just took a pencil. That says a lot about the Russians, to me.

Dimitry explained that the Russians sent more than 47 dogs into space in different missions, only 20 of them coming back. I heard that the Russians used stray dogs, from the streets of Moscow, because they would already be toughened up from living on the streets and used to harsh temperatures. The Russians successfully sent up two dogs in 1951. I say successfully; they got out of the earth's atmosphere, into space, but didn't make it back alive. It proved that a mammal could survive the launch and leaving the atmosphere.

Laika is the most famous of the Russian space dogs, because she was the stray that became the first living creature to orbit the earth in space when she was sent up with Sputnik 2 in 1957. Even though it was seen as a success by the Russian space agency, she died in space, from overheating. Both the Russians and Americans had been experimenting with mammals in the early days of space exploration since the late 1940s, when the United States sent up Albert II, a rhesus monkey, in June 1949. He didn't make it back. His name gives you a clue, but Albert I wasn't cut out for successful space travel either.

Laika is the animal nearly everyone names if they know owt about four-legged cosmonauts, but Belka and Strelka were the first two dogs to return from space alive, in August 1960. The Americans had more luck. Gordo the squirrel monkey made it all the way to space and back in 1958, but died when the return capsule's parachute device failed. What a bastard! Then, in 1959, a couple of monkeys, Able and Baker, made it back and survived, but Able died in an operation to remove a sensor. Baker lived on to the age of 27.

Dimitry took us through every area of Russian space travel, from Sputnik to the present day and their involvement with the ISS, the International Space Station. The USSR was the first country to put a man in space, on 12 April 1961. They kept talking about Yuri and, for a while, I thought they meant the spoon bender. Sorry, that's Uri.

Yuri Gagarin was a hero of the nation, son of a bricklayer, who worked loads of jobs to get enough money to earn his pilot's licence. He was only in space for an hour and a half. I say 'only', but no one had done it before, so after you, mate. He died in a fighter jet training crash, just short of seven years later, that many folk still think is mysterious.

Dimitry also told us about a Russian cosmonaut who spent the longest uninterrupted length of time in space: Valeri Polyakov was up there for 437 days, over 14 months. (Valeri was a bloke, by the way.) And he also told us that cosmonauts come back five centimetres taller than when they left because the lack of gravity in space means their joints and spines aren't compressed. The height increase doesn't last for long, though.

The last day of filming in Moscow was in the Metro, and what a beautiful place it is. Moscow's Metro is like nothing you've ever seen. Lenin started the job and Stalin finished it. They planned it as an example of how advanced the Communist Soviet Union was. The stations are beautiful, like art galleries, cathedrals or ballrooms, with marble-lined walls, massive chandeliers hung from arched and vaulted ceilings, huge mosaics on the walls and hundreds of statues.

The Russian people supplied the labour, and were worked brutally hard to make sure it was finished on time, but it was the British who supplied the know-how. Stalin got a load of British engineers in to design his underground, because the London Underground was the first, and, at the time, biggest underground network, but then the Russians didn't pay for any of the work. You can't build an underground system beneath a major city without getting to know the ins and outs of the place you're tunnelling under and this wasn't good in a place as paranoid as Stalinist Russia. The NKVD, the People's Commissariat for Internal Affairs, who were the secret police before the KGB, were used by Stalin to arrest anyone he had it in for, and they took in loads of the British engineers on suspicion of spying, just because they'd made it their business to know the layout of Moscow. I don't know how they could plan to build an underground system without that research. Anyway, they got away relatively lightly. They were tried before being deported to England, not sent to Siberia. That was back in 1933.

The materials used to build this massive engineering project came from all over the USSR, including the steel, cement, marble and granite. When you've got a land mass the size of the Soviet Union you don't have to import much from outside.

Stalin wanted the folk of Moscow to be convinced, or fooled into thinking, what a great regime they were a part of on every journey to and from work. He wanted to show that the Soviet underground was better than any in the West, so no expense was spared. Being Communist Russia, there weren't any adverts for soap powder or tobacco, like there would have been at King's Cross Underground in the same era. Instead, there are hundreds of works of art, all in the style known as social realism. It's a style showing the Russian people looking healthy and happy and staring optimistically into the future. Ordinary people like farmers, industrial workers and schoolchildren are the main subjects, pictures of the people at work in the fields, showing the country working together for each other, men and women. It's about the present and the future, not the past, to make people feel that it might be bloody horrible now, and you're short of food, but keep working, comrades: this is the future.

I thought filming for a whole day on the underground would be a bit much, but it is massive and was dead interesting. We were hopping on and off trains, going here and there. No one was gawping at us, no one was paying any attention at all. The first time I had to film anything in public, seven or eight years ago now, I felt awkward, but I'm used to it now. I've got over feeling like an idiot. I can just get on with it, but it is easier if no one, except the crew, is looking on.

Misha was guiding us, taking us to various places, sometimes leaving the stations and going out onto the streets. We didn't go to Russia to see the outside of the FSB headquarters, what was the KGB HQ, or any military stuff. We weren't there for the politics. We'd done a bit of Red Square and the Kremlin and that was enough. We wanted to see what made the place tick. We wanted to show the positive side of Russia, not the same old stereotypes.

When we're filming, I don't have a script. I never do. If you've seen my programmes, that won't surprise you. On a day like this Misha fills me in on the history, then James, the director, will ask me questions on camera and I'll explain what I've been told, picked up, seen or thought about.

One bronze statue stuck in my mind. It was in the Ploshchad Revolyutsii, Revolution Square, station and of a soldier with his arm around a dog. Loads of Russian folk who walk past it rub the dog's nose for good luck, so its snout is shiny. There are said to be 76 bronze sculptures in this one station alone.

What with hearing about Laika and the other space dogs, and seeing this statue, I was already beginning to miss my two Labradors, Nigel and Steve.

The final bit of filming for the day was for me to meet the owner of a ZiL, the presidential transport, a Cold War-era limousine. Misha arranged for us to meet the bloke, who called himself Vladimir. I don't know if he was an oligarch, but he wasn't short of a bob or two, and we know Vladimir wasn't his real name but I wasn't going to push it. I could tell by the way he dressed, his presence, that he was definitely a doer. So I ended up doing a lap of Red Square in a ZiL. It was mega.

That night was our last in Moscow for a while. We were never far from ten-foot icicles and you're deafened by the noise of studded snow tyres, but we'd been right in the heart of Russia and had no bother at all. The traffic is bad, worse than London, but, then, Moscow has a bigger population, over 12 million compared to less than 9 million in London. Walking around Moscow on my own didn't feel dangerous. There were no funny looks. I never felt threatened. I liked the place.

CHAPTER 13

'Arsehole checker, that was his full-time job'

DAY FIVE OF the Russia job was a travel day, flying from Moscow to Archangel, near Murmansk, nearly 700 miles north-west of Moscow. We didn't have any days off, we were either filming or travelling every day on this nearly four-week trip.

We landed in the afternoon and I did a piece to camera (PTC in TV jargon). James, the director, has the programmes planned as best as he can in advance, but we also have to react if something happens. As I've said, nothing's ever scripted. James has been doing it a long time, so he'll know if the programme needs an extra bit from me to help tie things together, and those are when I'll be asked to do a piece to camera. Not all of them are used, but it's better to have them and not need them. This one was about the Arctic convoys from 1941 to 1945, because Britain and Russia were allies in the Second World War. There were 100 ships and 1,000 men lost taking supplies of tanks, planes, tractors and food to the Russians through the back door, so they could defend themselves against the Germans moving east. Archangel and Murmansk were the main ports the convoys were sailing for, but the German navy and Luftwaffe knew it and would try and pick them off.

The main reason we'd travelled up there was to visit the partly state-owned Archangel diamond mine. Misha had been working hard to keep things on track because the plans were changing all the time. Places we were told we could visit changed their minds or said we couldn't have the access they'd already agreed to. We didn't know for sure, but we all felt it was down to the diplomatic problem over the Salisbury poisoning and things weren't quite as we expected when we rolled up to the mine, but James and Misha managed to work things out.

I was told this place was the biggest diamond mine on the European land mass, but I didn't realise Russia was part of Europe and when I said that people looked at me like I was a dickhead. I found out later that Russia is split into two anyway – European Russia and Asian Russia, and

The Kremlin, Moscow.

Version of the Caspian Sea Monster near Moscow, it flies off ground effect.

Russia. With some of the TV wankers, good bunch.

6x6, strange PTO set up, but a proper piece of kit.

Getting into the audiobooks.

Arctic Convoy memorial, to the 1,000 lost at sea.

As trick as trick, Kamaz Dakar racer.

Exclusion Zone – radiation sign off sheet

DATE __11/04/18__

Team Member	Entry time	Exit time	Daily Reading ṁSʰ	RPO sign to confirm reading	Team member sign to confirm acknowledgement of reading
Guy Martin	07.30	18.00	22·52		GM
James Woodroffe	"	"	19·51		
Nat Bullen	"	"	·18·90·	Thomson	Nm
Andrew Chorlton	"	"	3·00		
Max Burton	"	"	3·58	IA	
Mat Adams	"	"	2·11		
Aido Kane	"	"	2·60		
Stuart McGill	"	"	3·45		J.C.
Amy Roff	"	"	3·33		
Jessika Barcynski	"	"	2·10		
Dima Kolchinsky	"	"	2–29		
Iain Thomson	"	"	24·66		

Chernobyl, the most deadly place on earth, yet you wouldn't know it.

Hairy job, well prepared.

The Night Wolves'
back garden,
Moscow.

Cammy and Trellis, the original team.

Steve on
the sofa.

My girls.

Dot's first car, work
in progress.

there's a lot more of it in Asia, so I wasn't being totally stupid. Anyway, it's the biggest diamond mine in Europe, because it's west of the Ural Mountains, the range that splits Europe from Asia.

We drove to the mine on the morning after flying there. All the rivers and lakes in the area were frozen, with cars driving on the ice. A boat was frozen in. I wondered how long it had been stuck there. It was minus 20 here, much colder than Moscow had been. This was the only time I felt I didn't really have enough clothes with me, but I was all right. The crew had brought a load of cold-weather clothing, and I could've had it all bought for me, but I didn't, because I'm hard. I had my Pikes Peak woolly hat.

Archangel was the nearest town to the diamond mine, but it was still three hours' drive away, so it's pretty remote. The mine has its own power station. The people who work there do shifts of two weeks on, two weeks off. There's a sports hall, a swimming pool, a bar and a shop. It's a well-catered-for place.

The mine is open-cast, a big hole in the ground, not underground like you might think when you hear the word mine. They use a big Bucyrus crane, with a big Caterpillar V8 in it, that excavates in a certain way that claws the ground and loads the dumpers in fewer movements. Ruston-Bucyrus was a joint British-American company, with the British side based in Lincoln. It's just Bucyrus now and they make these massive diggers.

It maybe took six bucketfuls to fill the bed of a 90-ton dumper truck; 90 ton is what it can carry, and I got to drive one. I had 92 ton on the back and set off driving out of the mine. Even though it was the biggest thing I'd ever driven it felt very familiar, probably less complicated than my John Deere tractor. It's that big you have to keep an eye on a few screens, displaying camera angles positioned to help the driver see the corners. It had the choice of four gears, but it was a CVT system, constant and variable, with a hydraulic system that worked off oil pressure. When the engine got to this speed, it changed gear automatically.

On average, they reckoned, you get one carat of diamond for each ton of dirt that comes out of the ground. A carat is 0.2g. It's not exactly trying to find a needle in a haystack, but it isn't far off. They've refined the process, though.

There's no human contact until right at the end of the process. The 90-ton load gets tipped into the graders, where it is puckered up, until it gets sorted, then X-rayed and scanned by an ultra-violet light. Any diamond in there shows up under the ultra-violet light. There's an air system that blasts that certain part of rock out for further inspection. That piece goes through another heating process to get all of the moisture out of it, then into a clinically clean room where nine people are sat, dressed like surgeons, with hairnets, sorting through the rocks and stones they hope contain diamonds.

Obviously when the air blasts what it recognises as a diamond out of the mixture of rock and dirt there's only a small percentage of diamond; it's also taking normal rock with it. These folk are sorting the shit from the diamonds. The gems look like dirty glass at this point, all different colours: yellow, blueish, white.

I got all togged up to help look for the diamonds. You get checked in and checked out. You have your hair, earholes and arsehole checked to make sure you haven't hidden anything. All the windows are sealed so nothing can be dropped out. You have to get your shoes cleaned wherever you go. You put your shoes, still on your feet, through these machines to make sure you haven't hidden anything in the grips in the soles, and those machines are sealed so no one can hide something on their shoe, knowing the machine will find it, thinking they can just get it out of the cleaning machine later.

Everything was immaculate. The workers searching for the diamonds were lining up the stuff they were sifting through like I've seen people in films line up cocaine before they snort it. But they're doing it real fast. It's mostly women, with only one bloke in there the day we visited. And they have to get their arseholes checked on a daily basis, during the two weeks on of their shift pattern, too. There's a bloke whose job it is, arsehole checker, that was his full-time job. The folk who worked there weren't small.

There were a lot of places to hide a lot of things. They ran a fine-tooth comb through my hair.

I think we did well to get any permission to film there at all. They were that impressed with how into the whole process we were.

We also went to Alrosa, the diamond company's Moscow headquarters. We were told they'd never let any media see behind the scenes at this place, but they liked our enthusiasm. After Misha contacted them they'd agreed to let us in.

Nearly 30 per cent of the world's diamonds come from Archangel, and, according to their own figures, they extracted 37 million carats of 'rough' diamond in 2016 alone. They sold that year's haul for 317 billion roubles (the equivalent of about £4 billion at the time of writing this).

The final process, the next step on from the nine folks sorting them in a sealed room in Archangel, is where the company decides what they're going to do with the diamonds. Some might be too rough to be gems, so they use them for industrial purposes like grinding wheels and drill tips and that sort of stuff, then there's all different grades of jewellery.

For the diamonds that are good enough to become jewellery, Alrosa have a computer program to help them work out if they should leave it as one big stone or cut it into smaller ones. It also depends on the demands of the market. They had a big bugger there, the size of a good potato, still uncut. The Alrosa folk told me they've had it for six months, but they were still waiting to see what the market would do. They have meetings to decide what to do with it. It's rare to find one that big, so they could leave it as one big gem if they thought someone had the money to pay for it.

Once they've sussed out how they're going to cut any particular diamond they rough-cut it with a laser, a million-dollar Swiss machine, then polish it with a special abrasive wheel. They have a special tool that can hold the tiny diamonds and it's indexed so you can turn it for 6 degrees or 45 or whatever angle you want. I had a little go at cutting and polishing that. It was interesting and something I'd never really thought about before.

They had a group of five cut diamonds that they called the Alrosa Dynasty Collection, a world famous thing that they take to diamond shows all over the world. The five stones are cut from one 179-carat rough diamond the company recovered from one of their other mines, way out in the east of Russia, in 2015. The biggest cut diamond from this one rough diamond is 51 carat, 10g. Quite a thing. With so much about Russia, I hadn't thought of it as a diamond producer. Luckily there was no anal cavity search leaving this place.

After we'd finished at the diamond mine, we drove the three hours back to Archangel that night, got up the next morning for another travel day. This time we flew south-east to Moscow before getting a connecting flight to

Irkutsk in Siberia. It was a six-hour flight, with a six-hour time difference.

We landed in Irkutsk, at maybe eight in the morning, then went for a brew before driving to a railway yard on the Trans-Siberian Railway. The idea was to meet the permanent rescue team based here.

There are maybe 20 of these on the length of the railway, the longest in the world, each team covering summat like 200 miles west and 200 miles east of their depot. The trains don't break down, I was told, but they deal with derailments, springs breaking, livestock on the track, bogies coming off, trees falling onto the lines . . . They have a massive train with a 200-ton crane on the back to go and recover any derailed carriages or deal with anything else chucked at them.

The line is 5,722 miles long, starting in Moscow and ending up in Vladivostok, travelling through eight different time zones along the way. It pre-dates the Russian Revolution, going back to the time of the tsars. It made me realise how far the bicycle ride to Magadan will be. I want to ride through Siberia, so I thought I'd have to get to Moscow and go northeast, but Siberia forms all of the middle part of Russia. It borders China, Mongolia and Kazakhstan, does Siberia. I didn't realise almost the whole east of Russia was Siberia. They reckon that 9 per cent of the world's dry land is Siberia.

While we were there, the Russian crew practised fixing a derailment and replacing a bogie. Just watching them work was impressive. They let me do bits and bobs, but I could see they knew what they were doing. The temperature was a bit above freezing, so it wasn't the harsh conditions those boys have to go out in, halfway through a Siberian winter. The temperature can be minus 40 when the wind gets up, but it wasn't that cold when we were there. We had beautiful blue skies, and there was snow everywhere.

They let us get involved in a practice of how to deal with a derailment, how they get the train back on the track, how to fix the bogies on, how to change the bogies, use the crane. It's a practice they go through every couple of weeks. They're not messing about.

Trains carrying wood and container boxes were rattling by while we were working. They are massive. You can be waiting five minutes for one to pass, and they looked like 150 carriages long.

Again, they were lovely people and it was a good experience. How many British people have worked with a rescue crew on the Trans-Siberian Railway? I don't know either, but I'm guessing not very many.

The next day we had a long drive from Irkutsk into the Buryat region to visit a village and meet some of the local shaman-like folk. We drove on the main road out of Irkutsk for an hour before turning onto a dirt road for another hour and a half to get to the village. We were in the Asian side of Russia now, south-eastern Siberia.

The village was on the edge of Lake Baikal. This massive lake holds more freshwater than any other lake on earth, more water than all the North American Great Lakes combined. But it is over a mile deep in places, so while it holds more water, it is only the seventh biggest lake in terms of surface area. The bits we could see of it were frozen over, people driving on it, lads cutting holes in it to go fishing.

The Buryat we met weren't shamans, or I don't think they were. I reckoned they were just playing the part of how their previous 17 generations had lived. A shaman is someone believed to have an influence on or a connection to the spirit world, so I suppose it depends on your point of view if any of these folk were shamans or not, but they believed in it. When we arrived they had a welcoming committee singing and dancing in the traditional dress of long, bright, satiny type of robes and round hats. They looked the business, but don't normally dress like that; it was all part of the re-enactment to keep the traditions from being forgotten.

It had been arranged that I'd be involved in a couple of the important old traditions, the first being making alcohol from fermented milk.

We boiled up this cheese-like milk stuff. As it boiled off the steam condensed on the inside of this upside-down bucket thing with a shovelhead in it, ran down a spout and the liquid was caught, ready to drink. Or they reckoned it was ready to drink. To me it smelt like what it was – fermented milk alcohol – and it didn't taste much better than it sounds. The process took a couple of hours, but I can't remember a lot of detail, because I was pissed by the end of the day.

This vodka-like drink, that smelt of off milk, was used as part of a ceremony that they involved me in. Every now and then I'd get a nod and that meant I had to take a drink, and I ended up finishing a cupful. The crew had a drink too. Get your lips round that. We had to taste the fruits of our labour, after all.

During this ceremony they gave me this hefty bone, a cow's thigh bone or summat, and told me I had to break it. I said, 'Give it here,' and I was about to break it over my knee, when they said, 'No, no, no, you must break it like this,' and showed me I had to punch it with my bare hands. I had a go, but I told them I'd break my bloody hand if I tried that again. Stu and Aldo, the ex-Marine hardmen that came with us, they both tried and said, 'Fuck that!' Aldo reckoned he did break a bone in his fist, and he's a handy lad. The Buryat got in one of their sons, a big unit, and he did it, but it smarted him. Fair play to him. I was ready for a kip in the people carrier on the way back to Irkutsk.

The crew are all good people. They're not complainers. As long as they're fed and watered they keep on working till it's done. James, the director, was happy with the footage we were getting.

Day ten was another travel day, this time to Bratsk, where we were travelling to do some logging. Siberia had a lot more towns than I thought. Like I said, it's a much bigger area of Russia than I realised before I visited. Russia has a bigger proportion of area covered by forest than any other country. It has over 2.3 million square miles of forest; that's more than the land mass of the whole EU. I was told a third of the world's CO_2 is sucked up by Siberian forests. I was also told the forests are growing back faster than they're cutting them down.

We were supposed to fly from Irkutsk to Bratsk, but the TV lot weren't sure the plane would fit all our stuff on, so the plan changed to a ten-hour drive.

We did some nattering on the way. We'd stop at a level crossing, wait 20 minutes for the train to pass, and jump out to do some quick filming about the trains, talk about where we were going, talk about the USSR. The journey wasn't the worst. I looked out the window. Everything looked very Soviet here. I was talking to Misha and finding out more about Russia.

I'd been given an iPod for Christmas and finally managed to work out how to get it going and got into downloading podcasts. I listened to Garry Kasparov on *Desert Island Discs*. By now I'd met plenty of Russians and we'd had next to no bother, except for a few changes of plan. Nowt major, and nothing like we'd all imagined it would be before we landed. I'd built bridges in my head, thinking, It's all right is Russia and the way it's run. Then I listened to Kasparov. He was the world chess champion, a hero in Russia, where chess is a big thing. Born in 1963, he grew up in the USSR, in Baku in Azerbaijan in the deep south of the Soviet Union, but he's lived outside Russia since 2013, because, he says, 'Visiting Russia would be a one-way ticket.' He isn't a fan of Putin: he says Russia has a criminal regime and is a police state and that it's a 'one-man dictatorship'. He'd spent time in prison after protesting against Putin, who Kasparov says is a KGB dictator who has been involved in killing some of his journalist friends. On the Radio 4 programme I'd downloaded, Kasparov said, 'If you have only one restaurant in town serving only one dish, this dish is popular.' He said a lot by saying not much.

On the way to Bratsk we saw some lads playing cricket, or their version of it, with a ball and stick at the side of the road. We pulled over to speak to them. We'd done something similar when I was riding the Royal Enfield in India: just go and have a natter to them. They didn't have a proper bat, just a stick, but they were fit-looking, country kids, about 15 of them all between the ages of 10 and 15. I sat and watched for a bit, then asked them some questions through the translator.

They were in shorts, but there was snow at the side of the road. I asked what they were up to and they told me they were just mucking about. They seemed dead happy kids. A couple of them were about to leave school. One was going to be a welder, one was going to be a builder. None of the kids were saying they wanted to be famous or work in IT, there was none of that. I liked their enthusiasm for life, not that I haven't got that, but it was interesting to see their outlook on life. We talked about the World Cup coming to Russia and they were excited about that.

Back in the van I listened to an audiobook of Yuval Noah Harari's new book, *Homo Deus: A Brief History of Tomorrow*. I got four hours into it then lost it on the Cloud or somewhere. Harari wrote *Sapiens*, that I'd read a few years ago, and the new book was fascinating. Listening to different liberal views and how the measure of a country's happiness is the suicide rate. As a species, we're never happy. I learned that more people are dying from eating too much than eating too little.

We ended up at the hotel in Bratsk at ten at night. We were picked up early the next morning, and taken to Ilim, a paper pulp producer. They make something daft like 60 per cent of the world's paper pulp. The factory is massive. From there it was another three-hour drive to get to the area of forest they were felling at the time. There was a full team of workers there: mechanics, crane operators, truck drivers, everything you need to run a lumber operation.

The PPE – personal protection equipment – was a big thing there so I got a jacket, embroidered with my name in Russian, and a hard hat, then I could sit in on a bit of tree felling with the driver of a Finnish machine called a Ponsse. It was a very complicated machine. It grabs the tree, cuts it down, strips all the bark and branches off it, cuts it up into sections and loads it on the trucks in one fluid motion. You want to see it. Amazing thing.

Because it's so complicated, with dozens of knobs and switches, they have a simulator, exactly the same, back at the factory. New operators get used to the controls before they're let loose to start cutting down 40-foot pine trees that weigh more than a ton. I'd sat with the driver for an hour or so, so when I got in the simulator I got my eye in pretty quickly and I could do it. I love the idea of job like that, but it would be rubbish for getting stuff done in the shed, because of the two weeks on, two weeks off shifts.

Some of the felled trees are transported on trucks, but some are dropped in the river and towed down with tugs. They leave them floating in the water till they need them.

The factory has millions of tons of wood in their yard; you've never seen so much wood in your life. Even though we'd done all this travelling I was still up for listening. The bloke showing us around was called Alexei, one of the top managers. He told me that he and his daughter raced go-karts on the ice in winter and he'd come second in the local championship, so he was quite proud of that.

It had been a long day, and on the back of a ten-hour journey the day before, but Alexei, who'd been showing us around all day, invited us all out for tea. The crew were knackered, so I ended up going with James, Aldo and Amy. I could've done with getting my head down, but it was great. They'd made enough food for all of us; only half of us showed up, but they understood.

Alexei gave a speech saying that when all the politics are put to one side it's good to spend time with people who are interested in what you're doing and interesting themselves. Which, of course, is dead right. Then the vodka came out. I'm not much of a vodka drinker, but when in Rome . . .

The next day, day 12, was another travel day, first to Moscow then another connecting flight to Izhevsk, a place I'd never heard of but is the nineteenth biggest city in Russia. It's west of the Urals, so in European Russia, in the Volga region. It's famous for its industry and weapons manufacturing, dating back to when the Russians were preparing for Napoleon to invade, and we flew there for a visit to the massive Kalashnikov factory.

When it comes to a product, not a person or a culture, Kalashnikov is probably Russia's most famous export, and everyone knows the name of their AK-47. The A stands for Automatic Gun; the K is from the inventor's name, Mikhail Kalashnikov, and 47 is the year it was first manufactured. The AK-47 is the key to modern revolution and made killing people easy. They've sold over 70 million AK-47s, made in over 30 countries and supplied to over 100 nations' armies. The silhouette of an AK-47 is even on the official flag of Mozambique.

Mikhail Kalashnikov was a bit like the atomic bomb man, Oppenheimer: he saw his creation as a tool to defend his nation and blamed politicians for 'resorting to violence'. He was a Communist man of the people. He came up with a great idea, but it was all backed by the regime. He combined ideas from German and American guns to come up with his own.

They make loads of different rifles and guns there and they're assembled in this very modern manufacturing plant, as cutting edge as Jaguar Land Rover or any company you can think of. It has a floor of CNC lathes, mills and other machinery and, above, a floor of assembly.

The production line had had some money chucked at it. Considering who their customers are, I shouldn't have been surprised that everything was made with military precision. It's not a surprise to learn Russia is the biggest exporter of arms after America, but I hadn't thought about it before. Since Putin got in charge Russia has more than doubled its military spending.

After the tour they took us to the shooting range. I'd fired guns before, when me and my mates Gunster, Jim, Chris and his brother went on a road trip to America when I was 24. We went to a shooting range in Las Vegas and had a go with a .357 Magnum and you knew about that when it went off. At the Kalashnikov factory I shot a 103 and an AK-47. The rifles have a mechanism in them that counteracts the recoil. The charge that pushes the bullet out of the barrel is also used to move a piston to counteract the kick of the gun into your shoulder. It still gives you a belt, but not as bad as you'd think. I don't know how accurate you'd say I was. I hit the bit of paper, but I was letting rip. I was trying to empty a full magazine in one go without the gun knocking me off my feet, which takes some doing.

We were a full two weeks into the job when we turned up at the massive Kamaz truck factory in Naberezhnye Chelny. I've wanted to visit the factory, on the Kama River, since I read about it in a magazine when I was in New Zealand a few years ago. The story was about a Russian-built truck that had won 15 Dakar rallies against the best from the rest of the world, including Tatra, MAZ, Iveco, MAN and Renault. They're the seventh biggest truck manufacturer in the world, making over 40,000 trucks a year.

They didn't let us into the regular factory, but we visited Kamaz Master, the race team, who build the specific rally trucks. It's the target of most of the folk who work for the company to land a job in Kamaz Master. Get promoted to the competition side of things and you've made it. I was excited to be there, like a rabbit with two tails, checking everything out. Kamaz was the main reason I'd wanted to visit Russia all along.

The 4326 racing truck uses a Finnish chassis with a Swiss engine with Belgian suspension, a German gearbox, brakes and axle. The 1,000-plus horsepower, 16-litre, V8, Liebherr engine is also used as a crane engine. The German truck manufacturer MAN use a similar one, but with 650 horsepower, but you don't see many of them on the road. They're as rare as rocking horse shit.

It's a combination Kamaz has got working very well but it's still a massive team effort to go and win the Dakar. I have no interest in doing the Dakar on a bike – I'm not much of an off-roader – but I'd like to do it in a truck. These are four-wheel-drive, four-wheel trucks. Each truck needs a three-man crew, driver, navigator and mechanic, but each of them has to be able to do each other's job.

We were taken to the test track to have a go in this year's Dakar-winning truck. The track was in snow-covered woods with frozen lakes. We drove there in people carriers and when we got there the truck was waiting for us. I asked how it had got there and they told us that this year's Dakar-winning driver had driven the 2018-Dakar winning truck there from the factory. I was impressed.

The driver, Eduard Nikolaev, who has won the Dakar four times, was really humble, but very, very proud of the whole Kamaz success. He'd worked there since he was a kid. He was a mechanic originally, and he explained he was just a small part of the whole effort. I was told only Russians have ever been on the Kamaz team.

The racing truck weighs nine ton, but it's got 1,200 horsepower, with a normal 16-speed truck gearbox, so it moves. Eduard was jumping the bastard! In the cab you've got cooling fans, all the GPS and gauges, but it isn't comfortable. The Dakar is 14 days of racing and you'd know about it, spending that long in the cab of that truck at speed. It was brutal: the heat in the Atacama Desert, in fireproof suits, sat three abreast across the cab on top of a racing truck engine and the heat it's kicking out.

It was a good end to a part of the trip that involved flying here, there and everywhere around Russia. The next day we'd fly back to Moscow. We were 14 days in and had another 12 days to go, before we left for home.

CHAPTER 14

'He wore big spacers on the bottom of his shoes'

ANOTHER DAY AND another flight, this time from Naberezhnye Chelny back to Moscow. Every flight we took, and there were ten in all, we had to book in summat like 40 extra bags over our regular allowance, because we had so much camera and recording kit. Every bag cost at least £100. I wouldn't want the bill for that.

Most of the day was spent travelling, but we did a bit of filming on the bridge near the Moscow hotel just about what we'd learned up to then. It was another piece to camera. James spotted somewhere that would make a good background so we climbed out the van and were done in ten minutes.

We hadn't done anything to do with motorbikes up till now, but that changed on Good Friday when we met up with a motorbike gang called the Night Wolves. They are back-patch club, meaning they'd be compared to the Hells Angels. They're not riding around in hi-vis or replica leathers. They're unusual in lots of ways, compared to most bike clubs, because they have very close links to the Kremlin. Putin goes riding with them and turns up at their events. They get hundreds of thousands of pounds worth of funding from the Kremlin every year to help educate Russian youths, no doubt following guidelines from the Kremlin. They have very strong views on stuff. They're not sharing much of an inclusive message when it comes to gay rights. That was clear.

The day I met them, the Night Wolves were holding a press conference, but we met them at their clubhouse first. I was introduced to the leader, Alexander Zaldostanov, also known as the Surgeon. He was the one who'd be holding the press conference. He was a scary, authoritative bloke. Alexander demanded respect wherever he went by saying nothing, but he wore big spacers on the bottom of his shoes. I noticed that. He only wanted to be filmed from one side. He was raised in Sebastopol, in Crimea, and he's a Russian nationalist, proud of his country whatever it does. He always wanted Ukraine to remain a part of Russia and told me he thought that independence has buggered the country.

The Night Wolves' clubhouse was much more than that. They have a custom-vehicle building business. It's open to the public, and they do real good food, and put on shows over the Christmas period and all through the summer. The shows are aimed at families, and are exhibitions of the machines they've made, stuff like talking trucks; machines the size of buildings that move, like robots; massive army trucks with their cabs made into wolves' heads. These things are works of art, and more Mad Max than Mad Max.

At the clubhouse there are pictures all over the place of Alexander riding with Putin. The Night Wolves are all massive supporters of Putin and every year they ride somewhere, sometimes Ukraine or Poland or Germany, to celebrate Russia's military conquests and victories. When they go to Crimea, which was an independent republic before Russia moved back into it in 2014, they ride through Poland, and the Polish don't like it. The Polish government doesn't agree with Russia's aggression in the region, and might even be thinking they're next on the list, so a few of the bike gang got arrested last year on their ride through.

They planned to ride to Berlin one year to celebrate Russia's defeat of Germany in the Second World War, but they had their visas refused. They were accused of attacks on naval bases and natural gas plants in Ukraine when it was all kicking off between Russia and Ukraine, and in Crimea too. People don't seem to talk about the Night Wolves without bringing up their politics.

They'd heard of me, and I was a bit disappointed about that. I was embarrassed. What have I done to earn respect, riding around a bit of tarmac in a circle a bit faster than a few other people? How does that make me better than anyone else? But it did mean that when it was time to go to the press conference, they trusted me to ride one of their bikes, so I rode to the press conference with Alexander. I was on a Honda X11, the factory streetfighter with the Blackbird engine. Another bloke had a Harley. Alexander was riding a tricked-up modern Yamaha V-Max.

The press conference was a dead official-looking thing, with loads of film crews and 100–150 people in the room. I don't know if Alexander's mate Putin had pulled a few strings to get people there.

Because the TV lot were following in people carriers, travelling from the clubhouse, they couldn't keep up with the bikes, so they only arrived for the end. Until then I couldn't follow what was being said. When the translator arrived Alexander, the leader, was answering questions from the journalists. He was very calm, but talking in an

authoritative way. I couldn't understand what he was saying, but I knew, whatever it was, he meant it and he was
saying it with passion.

The translator explained later that someone in the press
conference was saying that they'd been on the rides with
the Night Wolves and they didn't need to go through Poland
and cause a load of upset. Alexander replied that he was
proud of his country, he was proud of what they'd done
and they, meaning Russians, I suppose, don't need to be
ashamed. It turned out, he told the bloke who made the
point summat like, 'You can ride where you want, with a
rainbow flag stuck out of your arse.'

I ended up riding back to the clubhouse with them, and
was shown Alexander's collection of bikes. He told me
about a big bike show they organise in Sebastopol, and that
I was welcome if I wanted to go. He said a British bloke
used to ride there every year with a motorcycle and sidecar
powered by a Daihatsu car engine. Alexander described it
as the most Soviet-looking bike he'd ever seen. The British
guy wouldn't sell it, even though he kept being asked, then
one year he told Alexander, 'I'm done with it now,' and it
became the pride of the Night Wolves' collection.

While nearly all of the civilian stuff we'd arranged to film
had gone ahead without a problem, there had been a couple
of cancellations that were down to the diplomatic bother
after the Salisbury poisonings. One example was the space
centre, where, as I've mentioned, we hadn't got the access

we wanted, but it worked out all right in the end. Back in Moscow it was obvious the original plan of me going up in a MiG was something not even Misha could sort for us. We'd been sent an email saying that foreign citizens would not be allowed into the Kubinka Air Base, where the flight was going to take place. Misha, proving he really was the best fixer we'd ever worked with, had got on the case and suggested another idea. A lot of former Soviet trainer jets were sold off at the end of the Communist era. At the end of the 1990s, the country had something like 800 of these planes they didn't need, or want, and some were sold to private companies. One of these companies offers passenger rides in their jet, from an airfield two hours' drive south of Moscow. Misha arranged for us to visit and for me to go up in it.

It wasn't a MiG, but the plane looked like what it was, an ex-Soviet Union jet trainer, a Czech-developed L-39 Albatros. The Soviets must have different opinions of the actual albatross than the British, to call it that. The design dated back to the early 1970s and was built until 1996. They built the thick end of 3,000 of them and they were good for 500mph.

I wasn't that pleased with the change of plan. It's one thing going up in a current military jet, looked after by the air force, but because this thing was now in private hands I wasn't that keen on flying in it. I don't know what I'm looking at, but I know how complicated these things are and what's needed, from the electronics side, to keep this thing in the air. Anything could go wrong with it and, if it did, it would be messy. I didn't say anything to the TV lot, but I'd decided I was going to have a walk around it and tell them I wasn't going up in it.

Brian, my inner chimp, was getting a bit revved up by this stage of the job. This was day 18. We'd been from here to there to there, and I hadn't had a sweat on or felt like I'd done anything physically constructive in all that time and I wasn't in the best of moods.

We rolled up to the airfield and it made me feel even more certain my gut feeling was right. It was an old knackered place. Then I started looking around this plane and realised it was mint. I got talking to the pilot, Vassily, who was ex-military, in his fifties, and I thought, He's still alive, so that's a good sign. I looked at the plane, looked at the pilot and watched his mechanic for a bit. I could tell he knew what he was doing too, and decided I'd trust them.

Vassily, the pilot, said, 'Are you all right for me to give it some?' I told him to go for his life. I hadn't had any breakfast that morning and hadn't eaten anything on the way there. Even though I'd been in two minds about the whole idea I'd primed myself. I knew if I was going to get in the jet, and he did go for it, I shouldn't have anything inside me wanting to get out in a hurry.

I climbed up the ladder into the cockpit and the way they strapped me in put me more at ease. The engines were started and we were off down the runway, Vassily dodging potholes – no joking – then woof! We were off and flying for three-quarters of an hour.

I've been in quite a few unusual planes as part of the TV job. I'd been in a stunt plane getting used to G-forces before the Wall of Death attempt and also in a two-seater Spitfire and taxiing in a Vulcan bomber. I knew this bloke wasn't messing. We were going fucking fast in the old trainer and pulling a lot of G. It wasn't as wild as the stunt plane, but it was wild. I probably would have puked up if I had eaten anything that day.

Before we took off, the film crew, through Misha, had said to the pilot, 'Get as low as you can over the runway so we can film a flypast.' The pilot looked at Misha and asked, 'Are you sure?'

No one had any idea, except the pilot, of course, how low he was willing to fly this thing. He can't have been more than a few metres off the runway, at close to 500mph. From my seat it felt that if my Transit had been parked on the runway we'd have hit it. I'm not kidding. You'd have never got away with doing something like that in Britain. Then he pulled back on the stick and we went into a climb, pulling 7G, seven times the force of earth's gravity. The training I'd had with Mark Greenfield, the stunt pilot, for the Wall of Death, all came in handy. I closed my lips tight shut, started blowing on the inside of my cheeks and tensing my legs and stomach, all to make sure I didn't grey out or lose consciousness. Then Vassily said I could take control of the plane, like it was the most normal thing in the world. He had me doing loop the loops in a Cold War jet trainer. Even after all the stuff I've done and all the opportunities I've been offered, I still can't believe some of these things are happening. When we landed it was one of those times I had to tell Brian to keep quiet. You cannot buy experiences like this.

Day 19 would be the last full day in Russia, and I spent it being attacked by dogs. We hadn't had a lot to do with the military, because it wasn't what the programmes were about. We wanted to see what normal Russian folk got up to, so one of the few military things we had anything to do with, other than the jet fighter and that was civilian-owned now anyway, was a place that trained dogs to be used by the armed forces.

I like owt to do with dogs, so even though I was ready for home by now, Brian was keeping quiet. The dogs were mainly German shepherds and I dressed up in one of those big bite-proof suits and a helmet before the handlers set a dog on me. It went for me a couple of times, took me right off me feet and marked me through the suit. It didn't draw blood, but I knew it had hold of me, that's for sure.

It was Easter Sunday, so the staff at the dog training place had put drinks on for us, sat us all down and gave us a bit of cake. We were in a big Soviet building that had been converted for its new use. They gave me a book of the history of dogs in the Russian military that they signed, lovely people. And that was the last job in Moscow.

Russia had been brilliant. The folk couldn't have been friendlier. Misha taught me loads about the place and its history. If we'd have been going home now, 19 days in, I'd have been happy, but we were heading to Chernobyl. And Brian wasn't happy.

CHAPTER 15

'There's stories of people being so poisoned by radiation that their eyes changed colour'

WHEN WE DROVE to the airfield to film the fighter jet thing we were probably only a five-hour drive from Chernobyl, not even that, but you can't get permission to cross the border from Russia to Ukraine because of all the bollocks going on with the annexation of Crimea. So we had to drive two or three hours back to Moscow, stay another night, then fly from Moscow to Warsaw and from Poland to Kiev, Ukraine.

At this point I'd had enough travelling. I wanted to go home and do some proper work and I'd half told the crew that much, saying I didn't feel I was doing anything constructive. They'd get pissed off when I said that, reminding me that this was their job. When they did, I'd tell them, 'Yeah, but you're working, I'm just fucking about, being a puppet on a string.' I get paid well for it, but there are times it annoys me because I feel I'm not doing proper graft.

One of the crew told me I was educating the nation and that wound me up even more. I thought, Don't give me that shite. I wasn't having it at that point.

From Kiev it was another three or four hours to Chernobyl, on fairly shit roads. We had a new fixer by then, a Chernobyl specialist called Dmitry. He was older than me, but a bit hippy-happy, bandana tied on his head, that sort of boy. Right from the start some of the TV lot were slagging off the new Ukrainian fixer, because he didn't have everything laid out on a plate for us. Part of it was we had all been spoilt by Misha, who everyone thought was the best fixer we'd ever worked with. I agree that Dmitry could've been better at some stuff, but give the man a chance. Ukraine is classed as one of the most corrupt countries in the world. It can't be easy getting everything set up 100 per cent. Sometimes you've got to wing it and work it out when you get there. I felt the crew weren't being polite, or some of them weren't. Then it made me realise that some of them are not polite as a rule, they just turn it on when they want something. This didn't help improve my mood either.

Another bloke had joined us by now, Ian, a radiation specialist from the UK. Like Aldo and Stu, he was another ex-military fella.

All the crew had been made to have specific training before the TV company's insurance would let us go into Chernobyl. In TV, every risk has to be assessed, whether it's visiting a factory or doing something like the Wall of Death record attempt. You can go ahead with it, but they want to know the risks involved, so if the shit hits the fan they have their arses covered and can say they did everything by the book, then point to all the paperwork to prove it. The radiation training was part of that process.

I'd missed the course when the rest of the crew went on it in England, because I had too much on at the truck yard and couldn't get the time off. I was going to be away for the best part of a month and there was a lot on. So, I had my training in Ukraine. That worked out all right, because it ended up being filmed.

The Chernobyl training could be summed up in a few lines: Don't wander off on your own; Don't touch this; Don't do anything unless Ian does it. The training took all afternoon, but I reckon it could've been crammed into half an hour, 15 minutes at a push.

After that we were ready to drive into Chernobyl's 30-kilometre restricted zone to have a look and get our eye in. There was a lot of paperwork flashing to get in.

There are people living inside the exclusion zone, perhaps a thousand spread over the countryside, who moved back when they were eventually allowed to. There's no industry so people are doing what they can to get by, growing their own veg, keeping a few livestock, the odd chicken or summat. They're mainly old women: babushkas, Russian for grandmas, is what they call them. Most went back illegally, some telling the soldiers who tried to evict them that they could shoot them if they wanted to, but they weren't leaving. These old women had been through so much in their lives in Ukraine before then, back in Stalin's days and in the Second World War, that a bit of radiation wasn't going to scare them off. They've been living in the exclusion zone for over 30 years now.

We spoke to Marie, a lass who lived there with her husband. As old as the hills she was. The TV lot asked if there was anything I could help her with. Her gate was dragging on the floor, so they wanted me to try and fix it for some TV bullshit. I pointed out that we didn't have any tools, or really anything we needed, and that they still wanted to do it pissed me off some more. Really, the gate wanted ripping out and starting again, not bodging up. I tried fixing it, but it was worse than when we started with it. This was an example of doing something for the sake of doing it and that's not what we tend to do. I know it's TV, so it's *all* done for the sake of it, but this was a prime example of TV bullshit. Brian was revving up.

After a couple of days in Ukraine, James, the director, said, 'We can't carry on like this.' I was just being awkward. One of them would say something and I'd tell them they were talking shit for some reason or other, rather than playing the part of a performing monkey, which I know I am. I was still pissing them off by saying I felt I was doing nothing constructive. I was being awkward for awkward's sake.

James came up with an answer. He'd got hold of a push-bike, an old knacker, and told me he thought I needed to burn some anger off. He said, 'Either do that or you can fly home tomorrow night.' So I got on the bike and I was all right. I needed to get a sweat on and do something. I appreciated that he came to the situation with tools to sort the problem – get your head sorted on the bike or fuck off home.

We were staying 20 miles down the road, because visitors can't sleep in the exclusion zone. Once I got the bike I'd take different routes from the hotel to the gatehouse where I'd meet the TV lot. I'd set off an hour before everyone else and get a bit of a sweat on. The roads were really bad, so the cars couldn't travel quickly.

On the first day I got talking to a bloke from Belgium who was part of a photography club who had travelled to Chernobyl and were milling around as we pulled up. As we spoke he was getting quite emotional about the horror that had happened 30-odd years before. I'd been there a few hours by that stage, and I'd been looking around in amazement thinking, Life's ticking along quite nicely, really. Then, almost in the next breath, I'm talking to this Belgian who's describing the devastation. It made me think, I don't see it the same way you do, to be honest.

Chernobyl is only famous for one thing, and that's the reason we were there: the nuclear power station explosion that happened on 26 April 1986, described as the biggest man-made disaster of all time.

The explosion was caused by a test gone wrong. The power station management wanted to see if they could run the reactor at a really low-power output, because they wanted to find out how the reactor would behave if there was a power cut, and if it would create enough power to keep the core cool and safe. They had tried to run this test a few times and they'd never completed it because, every time they did, a call from Kiev, 65 miles away, would come in, saying, 'We've got a big demand for power, we need more power.'

Chernobyl opened in 1977, and was extended with new reactors over time, so by the date of the 1986 disaster the newest reactor, No. 4, was six years old. On that day in April, they got halfway through doing this test, shutting the Russian-designed RBMK-1000 reactor down to its low state, when they nearly stalled it. This RBMK design was about as basic as nuclear reactors get, but thought to be safe enough that it didn't need expensive extra structures around it to protect it in the event of a failure. And this was after they'd had a partial meltdown of reactor No. 1 in 1982.

During the test there was a power surge and the workers panicked. This design of the nuclear reactor has 1,660 ten-metre-long graphite tubes full of uranium fuel. To control the nuclear reaction, boron carbide rods are raised or lowered in the huge bath of uranium. During the test the heat and pressure gauges went off the scale, the workers panicked and dumped all the boron carbide rods in the uranium to control it. This was supposed to slow down the nuclear reactions and lower the heat and pressure, but it did the opposite. Because of the design of the reactor, the uranium rods had come out of the graphite sheath, so wouldn't go back into their case (like the throttle was wide open) and it jammed and wouldn't shut off. Also, because this test was going on, a load of the safety systems had been turned off.

At the time, Chernobyl was the biggest nuclear power station in Ukraine and it was set to be the biggest in the world. They had nearly finished construction of the fifth reactor – it still has its scaffolding round it, all the cranes are in position, rusting since the day of the explosion – and they had planned to build a sixth and a seventh.

In their panic, the staff realised, 'Shit, it's going too fast now!' They had opened it too much, but the design is a bit shit and there was nothing they could do. The reactor began running away, uncontrollably. Because the reactor was wide open, this created boiling water and a steam explosion and this caused a nuclear explosion, as there wasn't enough water around the rods to keep them cool. It doesn't matter what buttons they pressed then, the thing was in freefall.

When it exploded it blew the 500-ton top off the reactor. The job was well and truly fucked. Fifty tons of uranium fuel was vaporised and blown into the atmosphere. Flames were shooting 600 metres into the sky. Another 70 tons of uranium and 900 tons of the radioactive graphite rods were blown out into the surrounding areas.

People didn't know what to do. At the time folk were picking up pieces of the graphite casings that had been blown out of the building. You could touch them, because they weren't hot, but anyone who did touch anything from the reactor was dead within days.

Only two people died in the initial explosion (it was nearly two in the morning), but the radiation starting killing people within days and eventually did for thousands. The radiation alters the hardwiring of the body and that can lead to cancer and all sorts of things.

The remains of the reactor were burning at 2000°C for ten days. It was like nothing anyone had had to deal with before, and this was Soviet Russia, so they weren't asking for help or advice from other countries. The outside world only knew anything might be up days after the explosion, when workers at a power station in Sweden started setting off the radiation detectors in their plant. They were highly contaminated. At first the Swedes thought a nuclear bomb had gone off somewhere, but when they checked more they realised it was more likely to be a power station. Swedish diplomats got on the phone to Moscow who denied it at first, then admitted something had happened at Chernobyl. Sweden got it worst, after Russia. Radioactive rain fell on the country, contaminating the land that reindeer grazed on, and reindeer meat was too radioactive to sell for a while after.

The Russians tried to smother the reactor fire by dumping sand and lead on it. The helicopter pilots who'd flown over the place, trying to put out the fire, died of radiation poisoning. Their friends have said they were buried in lead coffins, that were welded shut, so they didn't contaminate the ground they were buried in.

There's a famous picture of a plane flying 100 feet above the reactor. You can just see the wheel of the plane in the corner of the photo. There were three blokes on board and they lasted two days. The amazing thing about what went on there, with the rods and blowing the 500-ton lid off the reactor, was the explosion was 400 times more powerful than the atomic bomb dropped on Hiroshima, but there is still 96 per cent of the energy left in the reactor.

They brought in robots to try and work on it, but they kept breaking down so they brought in the 'biorobots', the reservist Soviet soldiers, who they used to shovel sand on the fire: 'Right, you've done your three shovels, go sit down for an hour.' But within a minute they were being blasted with lethal doses of radiation. There's film from the time of the 'biorobots' throwing on half a shovelful of stuff at a time. It's not even pissing in the wind, it's even more pointless than that and they're being subjected to radiation that will kill them. For what? They were doing their duty, these reservists, part-time soldiers who had other full-time jobs but were retained for times of emergency or war. And that was the end for most of them. There's stories of people being so poisoned by radiation that their eyes changed colour. Not all the biorobots died and I even met one. He looked fit enough, and I told him so and he thanked God for that.

They realised that smothering the fire wasn't putting it out, but it was causing it to burn through the concrete of the reactor. If it kept burning, it would reach the solid ground, the bare earth the power station was built on, and then it would heat up the water table so fast it would explode and then the other reactors would blow. Miners were brought in from all over Ukraine to dig around reactor No. 4 to allow liquid nitrogen to be poured in to freeze the ground, while they thought of a better plan. The miners were working by hand, because scientists were worried power tools would affect the stability of the place. All Russia's liquid nitrogen was sent to Chernobyl, but by the time it was finished the reactor's core temperature had dropped to a safe level. All the miners who worked there died of radiation poisoning.

They reckon half a million men and women worked on the recovery, repair and sealing of the reactor and the contaminated area over the next few weeks, months and years, many of them being poisoned with unsafe amounts of radiation. It was just lucky that Ukraine wasn't wiped off the map. I've heard that Ukrainian experts say we were lucky the whole of Europe wasn't seriously contaminated.

We were in the Chernobyl area for six days, but we were never short of stuff to do. We spent a couple of days with Simon, an English bloke who was part of the international group, the EBRD, the European Bank for Reconstruction and Development. The EBRD raised €2.2 billion from a load of different countries to make a structure, called the New Safe Confinement (NSC), to contain the site and radioactive material in it. He knows the job inside out and he's in charge. He gave us the facts of the job in hand now, what they were doing to make it safe, how much the arch-shaped steel structure that contains the site cost, how long it took to build, how long it took to put in place, what radiation it's stopping.

The arch is something else. Because of the danger to workers from the radiation that's still there, they couldn't build it over the reactor on site, so it was constructed hundreds of metres away then moved into position when it was partly complete. It's the world's biggest movable land-based object, weighing 3,600 tons. It's 162 metres long and over 100 metres high and is now in position over the sarcophagus the Russians built more than 30 years ago.

It was reactor No. 4 that exploded, and No. 3 has been stopped, but it kept putting out power until 2001. It still hasn't been decommissioned yet. All this material has millions of years of half-life and they don't know what to do with it.

Simon was a brilliant bloke and with Ian he explained the different types of radiation. Alpha rays can be stopped by paper, beta rays by a big bit of steel, but you aren't stopping gamma rays unless you've got depleted uranium or a fair thickness of lead. They'll kill you. The other ones will kill you, too, but they're easier to stop. Then there's stuff like polonium-210, a radioactive metal that is harmless if it touches your skin, but if you ingest it, it will screw you over, like it did Alexander Litvinenko, the former Russian secret service officer who defected to Britain and was poisoned, with polonium-210, in 2006.

I climbed up to the top of the arch, 100 metres of stairs up the outside of it, measuring radiation with one of the Russian workers on the way up. The radiation was much stronger about two-thirds of the way up, where it was in line with the top of the ruined reactor. The Russian bloke was not keen on staying up there for long. Next we went right inside the arch, and saw the steel block sarcophagus that was built to contain reactor No. 4. Everyone was aware of how much radiation was being emitted and that we could only stand in this spot for 30 seconds, but we could stand in a different area of the reactor building for a minute. I had to stand in a particular place and not any closer. Now the arch is up they can start using remote-controlled machinery to dismantle the reactor.

I went into reactor No. 3 and stood on top of it, where the rods would have been. It's safe, for a few minutes at least, but the uranium that has been taken out of there is still in its wet state, which is not ideal really. It needs to go through a special drying process, then it can be stored and left alone. They just haven't gone around to it, they've had a lot on.

Chernobyl is the place where the power station was built, but that was never the main town in the area. The new town of Pripyat was built to serve the power station and benefited from the work there, and that's deserted now. It's just over ten miles from Chernobyl and it wasn't until two days after the explosion that most of the folk were evacuated, tens of thousands of them. They were told they'd be able to return, and not to take anything with them, but no one has, except the few old people. It's still fairly radioactive. Some say it's not going to be properly safe for human habitation for 24,000 years.

Pripyat has been ransacked. There are cordoned-off areas now, but there didn't use to be and it has been looted. The coppers could work out what came from there easily enough, because they'd go around the car boot sales and markets with Geiger counters, and find the stuff riddled with radiation.

We went into some big tower blocks that I don't think we were really supposed to go in and every room had been stripped bare. All of the flats were exactly the same, and none I saw had a separate bedroom. They had a kitchen, bathroom, a main room and some had a balcony, but there was fuck-all of any use left.

A fairground had been built for the town, with a big Ferris wheel, and it was going to open on the May Day holiday, but it never did, for obvious reasons. There's a dodgem car ride, and all the cars are there, but the electric motors have been nicked out of them. Everywhere is overgrown, and now no one lives there the town is supposed to be full of wildlife. They reckon elk, boar, deer and wolves are all doing well. Bears have been spotted in the area for the first time in over a hundred years and European bison and lynx have been reintroduced. I didn't see any of that, but I saw a load of Przewalski's horses, Mongolian horses that went extinct in the wild, but are doing well now the breed has been reintroduced from captivity into the exclusion zone. Even though there's all this talk of an increase in wildlife, I reckon if you left Caistor and the surroundings to go wild, there'd be a load more animals mooching about than what I saw in and around Chernobyl. And there are examples of mutations on the wildlife in the area, from the insects, through birds to bigger animals.

There are hundreds of stray dogs in the exclusion zone, too, because the residents weren't allowed to take anything with them, including pets. A day and a half after the explosion they got 1,200 buses in and shipped out the whole town and surrounding villages and said, 'Don't worry, we'll have it sorted in two or three days.' Thirty years later ...

Not long after the evacuation marksmen went in to shoot the dogs, but they obviously didn't get all of them because the descendants of those original dogs hang around where the humans are. They're all dead friendly. There are loads of people there, thousands working in and around the exclusion zone, and some have made shelters for the strays. The dogs eat whatever the humans chuck out. They got a good feed when I was there.

I spent time with Tim Mousseau, an American biologist who was there to research how the animals were dealing with high background radiation for a long period of time and what affect it was having on them. He's been doing this research for eight years. He's found out the dogs are dying earlier than he would expect. They only live about three years. Even though the weather was mint when we were there, ten to fifteen degrees, the shorter lives of the dogs is as much to do with the harsh winters and hot summers as the radiation.

Tim and his organisation put ear tags on the dogs to keep tabs on them, and whoever catches them takes the GPS-registered tags off and downloads the information to see where they've been. To catch the dogs they use a Ukrainian vet to shoot the dog with a dart from a blowpipe, like someone from the Amazon. He was a dog man. I can tell a dog man, and I could tell he had a lot of compassion for these strays.

During the filming, one of the TV lot went up to him and said, 'We want Guy to shoot the dogs.' When I heard that I said, 'You can fuck off!' It wasn't Brian speaking, it was me. 'I don't know what I'm doing. I'm not going to try shoot a dog with a dart!' Later I told them that they shouldn't be saying that. It doesn't matter if it's for TV; they're dogs, and we don't fuck about with dogs. A vet can shoot them, because he knows what he's doing, but I don't. James explained it wasn't meant like that, but if not then I don't know how they meant it. I'm happy to fly a jet, but you don't mess with the dogs.

So the vet shot two of the Chernobyl dogs, knocked them out, and I helped lift the pair of them to where he could examine them and do everything he needed to do. He was brilliant with them, dead gentle. One of them had a really manky ear, so he cleaned that up, while I was picking ticks off the other one. But they were fit dogs, and dead friendly. The vets are neutering them as they go along, to bring the number of dogs in the area down to a population the non-profit organisation that looks after them can deal with. The dogs mainly live around the guard posts. They look a bit wild, a bit husky-ish, but don't show any aggression. They obviously know which side their bread is buttered.

Right near the end of our time there I went on patrol with the dedicated police force that guards the exclusion zone. I'm not totally sure who they're guarding it from, probably tourists and maybe a terrorist threat, too; because of the spent fuel storage warehouse that is more of a concern. The main reason they have checkpoints is to make sure radioactive material is not taken outside the zone where it could contaminate clean areas. They have caught folk in there, though.

We did the patrol on motorbikes, Chinese things, based on Honda CG125s. The guard was checking the fence where looters had entered in the past. Everything was very routine: we do this at this time and we check these things. It made me think that it wouldn't be very difficult to get in, if you were determined, but would it be worth a Kalashnikov bullet in the ear if they thought you were a Chechen terrorist?

That was it. We were finished and everyone was ready for home. Brian had been unreasonable, but I still think he was right. I'm not doing the TV stuff to educate the world, I'm doing it for selfish reasons. I get these fantastic opportunities to do these amazing things, but if you ate your mum's Sunday dinner every day of the week, it wouldn't be the same. I'm doing the best things in the world, money-can't-buy stuff, and being paid to do it, too, but after three weeks I've still had enough of it.

I know if we'd come home straight after Russia it would have been all right. If there had been a month's gap, then back to Chernobyl, there wouldn't have been a problem. All right, I was being unreasonable for the sake of being unreasonable, I know I'm a performing monkey, but don't treat me like a dickhead.

As ungrateful as that sounds – and I do remind myself about all the stories I already have to tell Dot in the future – there are still times I'd rather be at work.

I also remind myself that I've earned a bob or two out of the TV job, but I've stuck to my rules. I've never once believed the hype, I've never thought I'm anything special, I've always stuck to what I was before this all started. I've always gone to work. I've always had daft hobbies. Those things have been the constants all the way through my life. As soon as I start thinking things like, I'm going to teach the nation – check me out . . . That will be the beginning of the end. Start thinking like that and the thin end of the wedge is in.

CHAPTER 16

'Honesty Tourette's'

THE WAY BRIAN, the inner chimp, flared up at Cherno-byl, how I reacted and thought about it later, made me realise that one of my problems is I've got honesty Tourette's. If I think something needs saying, I'll often say it honestly and bluntly, not try to sugarcoat it.

I was talking to a mate about the whole shooting the dog thing and that I thought some people I've been dealing with are only polite when they want something. He asked if I thought I was being rude to the TV lot when I ran out of patience in Ukraine, but I explained that I didn't think I was, because I was telling the truth. They were all doing their jobs, but I felt I wasn't doing anything constructive. I don't mean in the time between filming. I include filming, too. My mate pointed out that someone can be truthful and rude at the same time, and that's when I realised it's one of my problems.

The TV stuff has been great in many ways. It's opened up a lot of doors, made me a lot of money, but it could all stop tomorrow and it wouldn't bother me. I don't have a rock-star life, and I don't need it. I've never needed it. People say to me, 'Oh yeah, but you wouldn't have this or you wouldn't have that.' What they don't understand is I don't need those things, I just bought them because I had money coming in and I could. I wasn't going to get all the money in a pile and start swimming in it like Scrooge McDuck. I'm not like that. If the money's there I'll spend it, don't you worry, but if it isn't I'll live within my means.

If the TV lot want to do a five-year deal and build me a dyno room, they can, that's spot on, thanks, get cracking. If they don't, that's all right, I've got a mate in Grimsby with a dyno and I'll get by. I don't need it, and the thing is I don't crave any of these things, either. I've never wanted to be famous or wealthy.

I've got a nice house, but I was quite happy in the house before that, and I was happy renting my mate's little house next to the chippy in Caistor, before that. Yes, I have got a lot of stuff, I'm not denying it. I've got some stuff that I'm hoping is going to earn me a quid or two over the years, like the tractor and the pub.

When I put a full week and overtime in I'm earning £1,000 from the haulage firm. Sharon calls me a greedy bastard. Another mate told me it was my equivalent of the hair shirt. The hair shirt is what religious fundamentalists would wear to make sure their life was miserable, to remind themselves that Jesus died for their sins. It was popular for a while, but didn't catch on. Now, a hair shirt is used to describe self-sacrifice, making things unnecessarily hard for yourself for some personal belief. I don't need to work long hours on filthy truck engines, but I want to.

A big part of it is the sustainability. If everything stopped tomorrow, I mean the TV and all that stuff, I could carry on working on trucks and survive. That's why I've kept a 1999 VW Polo that my mate Mad Adrian gave me after he blew the engine up. When it all goes to shit, I've got that to fall back on and to get around in.

But that's not all of it. I keep saying it, but I'm not sure if anyone really listens: the trucks are still the only thing that give me job satisfaction. Building bikes gives me satisfaction, but that's my hobby, not my job. I'm having to pay to do that stuff.

For a long time I've thought that the TV lot would find me out, realise I am no good at it and it'll all stop, but I've been doing it for nearly ten years now and they've signed me up for another five, so I must be doing summat right, so why change what I'm doing? I could be doing more in my shed, but so what if it takes me a year longer to finish the pickup than if I wasn't working on the trucks?

The TV company has never said to me, 'Look what you've got because of us,' and they never would. They know, I hope, that I can't be held to ransom. It's not about the money, it's about the opportunity and I'm grateful, even though I don't always show it.

I've written in an earlier book that I went to see a psychologist (or maybe a psychiatrist, but I think a psychologist) in Ireland, because my girlfriend at the time felt she was pissing in the wind. All the whinging that she was doing to try and change me and I didn't give a fuck. She told me it wasn't human to react the way I did, so there must be a reason I was reacting like that. It was more for her benefit that I went and was diagnosed with something.

My lack of empathy was doing her head in. If she could put that down to something wrong with the way I was wired up, then she could deal with that, because it was me, not something she was doing. So I was diagnosed, with Asperger syndrome, and it made not one atom of difference to how I went about things.

It gave it a name, and that's the way things have got to be nowadays. If you're a bit different or you deal with things differently; if you deal with situations in a way that's not seen as normal, whatever the normal way is, then you have to be labelled. You've got Asperger's or some other form of autism. I think it's a load of shite.

I came away thinking, I appreciate everything you're saying and that's great, but what a lot of bullshit.

I don't give a fuck. It's not like I'm strutting around, saying 'I don't give a fuck.' I just don't give a fuck. It sounds right dismissive, and I'm not like that, but I don't give a fuck.

If there's one person who has honesty Tourette's worse than me, it's Sharon. She says some things and I think, You're not seeing the whole picture there because you don't have the full facts to hand. But she's saying it as she sees it. I realise I'll be in the same position, saying stuff that other people don't agree with, because we're seeing it from different perspectives. I wish everyone had honesty Tourette's.

The disagreement in Ukraine won't change how the TV lot and I work with each other. No one's going to plan a trip that long again, but for everything else we'll just get on with it. I put my Tour Divide head on. Just deal with it.

Ten years ago I was a mechanic who raced motorbikes and loved working in my shed. I still am.

CHAPTER 17

'It's going light over the crest, scratting for grip at 175mph'

THE TV LOT are often scratting around trying to think of ideas for shows for me to make. Before leaving for Russia, Ewan, one of the two directors I usually work with, asked, 'What are you up to? What are you doing with that Trannie?' I said, 'Nowt, really, I just got it back out of the

Grampian Transport Museum, in Aberdeenshire, that was borrowing it and I'm going to race it while I get my pickup done.'

The pickup I'm building, that's based on a Ford Escort Cosworth that I bought off my mate Mark Walker, is going to take a lot of thinking about. The plan is to race it at Pikes Peak in 2020 and I want to use as much cutting-edge technology in it as I can, torque vectoring, the whole lot, and I want to do as much of it as I can myself, so that's going to be at least a year or two's job.

In the meantime, I had made my mind up to race the Trannie, FT13 AFK. Before I could race it, I planned to fit a better gearbox; the one that's in it is not good for racing. I want to make it look a bit smarter and finish some bits off more to my liking, because it was finished in such a hurry to ship it out to America to race in the 2016 Silver State Classic, the top speed-time trial on the public roads of Nevada.

Krazy Horse, the motorcycle and car dealership in Suffolk, who did the lion's share of the original modifications, were brilliant, and all the credit is theirs. The lads at Ford Dagenham had already been messing around with a Ford Tourneo, a Transit minibus with a V6, and when they found out about the TV show and our plan they gave their project van to us to get the gist of the job. The working out they'd already done saved a load of time and head scratching, then Krazy Horse fitted a souped-up V6, from Radical, the Peterborough-based sportscar company. Krazy Horse were working to a tight deadline and brief, and what they made did the job. It raced at the Silver State Classic, no bother, but there was a lot that I wanted to re-engineer and make a neater job of.

All my thoughts about modifying and racing the Transit came good after it arrived back from America. At first I didn't want anything to do with it. I nearly sold it, because I didn't have room to keep it in the shed at my previous house, then it went to the museum in Scotland. I had no interest in it, because I had bugger all to do with the building of it. It was the first Transit I'd owned myself, so it still meant a bit to me, but not a lot, until I came up with the idea of sorting it for the 2018 Time Attack Championship and putting a bit of myself back into it.

Time Attack began in Japan in 1994, as a challenge between the Skyline and Supra tuning businesses, at the Tsukuba Circuit. The Japanese had a whole tuning industry making mental horsepower road cars. All these tuners were saying my car does this, my car does that, so someone had the idea of getting them all together at one track to see who could do the fastest lap on that day, and that's where it started.

The Time Attack idea came over here and started as a recognised series in 2006. It's a time-trial race series held on regular short circuits, like Donington, Brands Hatch or Cadwell Park, and is growing in popularity. Each driver is on track on their own, competing against the clock, not starting from a grid like a regular race. The big appeal for me is the format of the rules: there aren't many. You can do pretty much what you like, as long as you tick the safety boxes. There are different classes to suit different folks' budgets, but you don't have to fit into narrow boundaries that make all the cars look the same. In the Pro and Pro Extreme classes you can go as daft as you like, fit the biggest turbos, use whatever car you want, fit slicks, spend as much as you like, go mental. I love the idea of that.

It appeals to me more than regular starting-on-a-grid-and-racing-to-the-flag short-circuit racing, because Time Attack is more about the building than the racing. Getting the Martek ready to race at Pikes Peak in 2014 made me realise that I enjoyed all the preparing, refining and problem-solving involved in getting the Martek to the start line more than the riding. I like the riding, or the driving, but it's only part of it. And Time Attack will let virtually anything race.

I was properly introduced to Time Attack by Phil Reed, someone I've known through racing for a few years. He ran East Coast Racing, the road racing team that the Irish racer Lee Johnston rode for. I've known him for a lot longer than that because I rode one of his Honda RC45s for *Performance Bikes* magazine about ten years ago. He's in his early forties, so he must have only been in his early thirties when he was letting me ride his RC30 and RC45. He ran a construction business and liked spending his money on bikes.

Phil competes in Time Attack's Extreme Class, the anything-goes class, and has done for a couple of years. I'd say his Mitsubishi Evo VIII is the best car competing in the UK series. I went to watch him race at Cadwell and he told me there was one meeting, at Croft race circuit in North Yorkshire, during the 2017 season he couldn't do, but his sponsors wanted the car out there, and he asked if I wanted to race it. Too right I did. I just needed to sort out my racing licence, an MSA National B licence.

To get the licence I had to do an ARDS (Association of Racing Drivers Schools) test. I did one ages ago, but I needed a refresher course, a total of three hours driving a sportscar around a track with an examiner beside me. Phil said he was hiring Croft with some other racers, so he could test his Evo, and told me I could borrow his road car, a Porsche GT3 RS, a £140,000 race car for the road, to do the ARDS course in. What an honour that was. He's a trusting man.

The Porsche had all the electronics that would save me from a bomb scene if it all went wrong and the car's trick traction control system did save me a couple of times. I was licking on and did enough to convince them to give me a licence.

I'd done a load of laps in the Porsche, and that's a car I reckon would be quicker than a Bugatti Veyron around a track, in the same league as a Porsche GT2 RS or a McLaren. The Porsche is as fast a production car as you could ever buy.

Then, at the end of the day, I had a few laps in Phil's Time Attack Evo to have a feel for what I would be driving in the race. It's a souped-up version of a £30,000 road car, and I went six seconds a lap quicker straight away than I did in the Porsche. So I'm obviously not shit; I've got half an idea of what I'm doing behind the wheel, but that's how good that Evo is. Six seconds is a massive difference.

The motorcycle lap record around Cadwell Park is 1:26 or summat. Driving his Evo, Phil Reed did a 1:25 around the same circuit, so he's faster than the fastest ever British Superbike. At Croft I was lapping faster than British Touring Cars, that's how good this car is, even though it's still a Mitsubishi Evo and I'm no professional driver.

I did a few laps around Cadwell at a track day in March 2017, six months before I would race it, too. When you're going up Cadwell's back straight there's a bit of a crest, but you don't notice it on a motorcycle, because you're already on the anchors. The braking points are all different in a car and, because you can brake so late in this car, it's going light over the crest, scratting for grip at 175mph. That's what impressed me the most. You compare it to one of Porsche's finest road cars, the GT3 RS, on slicks, and the Evo is seconds a lap faster.

It's a Mitsubishi Evo VIII, with all the weight possible taken out. It has the original cylinder head, but the bottom end is out of a Mitsubishi people carrier, so it has a longer stroke and is increased in size from 2.0 to 2.2 litre. It has a big eff-off turbo and nitrous, to mask the turbo lag. It runs on 120-octane fuel, has fancy suspension, a Bosch Motorsport ABS and a sequential gearbox. There is no interior except a driver's seat and roll cage. All the ECUs are mounted where the passenger seat would be. It races on slick tyres, makes 800 horsepower, when it was about 300 out of the showroom, and is a hell of a thing.

The Evo is so good you don't need any finesse with it. Just press the brake as hard as you can, as late as you dare, and the Motorsport ABS sorts it all out for you.

At the start of September 2017, I went back to Croft to compete in the race Phil couldn't make it to. Like a few British tracks, it is a former Second World War air base made into a race circuit. It's flat, but it's fairly fast and flowing and, for some corners, you have to be fully committed in fifth gear, 150–160mph in a car like Phil Reed's.

I was racing against similar stuff, souped-up Subaru Imprezas and Mitsubishi Evos, with about a hundred entries spread among the five classes, from hot hatches upwards. And I loved it.

You don't really get a sessions or grid start. You get four 20-minute sessions, and you're on track with cars from the same class as you.

You go out and do a steady lap to warm up, then one flying lap, then one lap to cool down. You need to find a clear bit of track, because you don't want to be held up by slower cars. Then you put your headlights on, so the other drivers know you're on a flying lap. That way, if you catch up to someone they should let you past. It's very gentlemanly: you're not out there rubbing door handles, like you sometimes are in a regular circuit race. Then you come back into the pits to watch the timing screens to see how your lap is comparing to those of the other drivers, while keeping an eye on the clock to make sure you don't sit out the rest of the whole 20-minute session. I had the best car and was quick enough in it to win the class by a good bit. What does that prove? If you can ride a bike, you can drive a car. It's not rocket science, is it?

I was keen to do some more of Time Attack, and realised I had this Transit with a mad engine in it doing nothing. It isn't the most sensible idea and definitely not the obvious choice. It's a van with six times more power than when it left the Ford factory, but it would be a good laugh. Making it work is all part of the challenge. And, as you know, I love Transits.

But all that was before the chat with Ewan, the TV director, about the plans for the van. I wasn't fishing for help or hoping the TV lot would be interested in what I was doing. The opposite, in fact; I was just making conversation. A few days later Craig, one of the North One lot and a proper car nut, came back to me and asked, 'What about trying to break the lap record for commercial vehicles around the Nürburgring?' Breaking a record around there has been on my to-do list for a while. I even wrote about it in *When You Dead, You Dead* so I said, 'Why not?' With hindsight I might have said it a bit too quickly, without really thinking hard about what it involved and what difference it would make having the TV lot involved in the job. Getting the Transit ready to compete in the Time Attack series was all about me doing it at my own pace, with my own money and ideas, with no one else involved. Now that had changed.

The Nürburgring Nordschleife is a 12.9-mile-long public toll road in the forests of western Germany. There's a modern short circuit, also called the Nürburgring, but I'm not talking about that.

The Nürburgring was built in the 1920s. It was used for Formula One races up until 1976, but a few fatal accidents, and Niki Lauda's infamous fireball accident in 1976, made the car racing authorities think twice about the place.

They still race saloon cars around there, including a 24-hour endurance race, but for the majority of the year it's a one-way toll road with no speed limit that road-legal cars and bikes can belt around. It's rented out to companies, too, for organised track days, schools, testing and photography as well. As long as it's not booked out, you can turn up on anything road-legal, pay your toll fee – that was €25 midweek, €30 for a weekend when I wrote this – and do a lap. On a public day everything's out there, from Porsche Carreras and Superbikes to coaches full of tourists. As you can imagine, there are a lot of crashes there.

Over the years I've spent a few days getting my eye in at the Nürburgring, but I've never got to the stage where I felt I could go for the record on a bike and confidently beat the 7 minutes 10 seconds motorcycle lap record. I had been thinking about it seriously, at the back end of 2014, early 2015. I was just going to take a bike out in a van, then the TV lot got involved and it all became a lot more official than just turning up in a van, paying the money and going for it. Once it had become a TV production it wasn't long before the Nürburgring authorities pulled the plug on it, saying they didn't want to publicise motorcycle record-breaking. I can sort of see where they're coming from, but they still run the place as a speed limit-free road and profit from people going balls out round there, so it seemed a strange time and place to draw a line in the sand. It's not like doing fast laps at the place is a big secret: that's the whole point of it. Anyway, they put a stop to it, but it was still on the to-do list.

The van record isn't the same as the bike job, but it's still something to have a go at. The current record is held by Dale Lomas, someone I met through *Performance Bikes*. He was a writer and road tester for the magazine when I used to do a lot of stuff with them. Dale got so into the Nürburgring that he moved to Germany. Now he's one of the instructors in cars and one of the Ringtaxi drivers – someone trusted to take paying punters as passengers on flying laps around the track. You can sign up to be driven around by an expert who is licking on, in a fast BMW saloon. Dale is not a messer round there. He knows what he's doing and there won't be many folk in the world who have driven, or ridden, more laps.

The TV lot knew Dale because they had made a programme with Paul Hollywood, the *Great British Bake Off* bloke, about car culture in different European countries. During the filming of the German episode they went to the Nürburgring and Dale took them on a flying lap in one of the Ringtaxis. They got talking to him and found out about this record. Craig, from the TV lot, told me, 'Dale wants you to break his record.' I couldn't help screwing up my face as I told him, 'Does he hell! Who holds a record and wants to have it broken?'

Then one of the TV lot said, 'Why don't you have him in the passenger seat?' The honesty Tourette's kicked in again and, without thinking, I said, 'Fuck off! He's fat as fuck! Why do I want him in the passenger seat?' Then I remembered, he's lost a load of weight, but anyway, even if he was seven stone, why do I want to be carrying any more weight than I need to? That van is heavy enough as it is, much heavier than standard, because of the massive roll cage and all that welded into it.

To break the record Dale had been supplied a VW Transporter that had been tuned and modified by UK VW specialists Revo. He broke the record set by another Ringtaxi driver, a German woman called Sabine Schmitz. Her record had been filmed for *Top Gear*. She did it in a fairly standard Transit, with a time of 10 minutes 8 seconds – from Bridge to Gantry. That means it was done on a public day when it's not possible to do a full flying lap because you have to pull off the track and into the car park before you complete a full lap. The van Dale drove was a used Volkswagen twin-turbo Transporter, with a remapped ECU, new exhaust, intercooler, new suspension, alloy wheels, sticky rubber. Revo reckoned it made 220bhp. Dale did a full lap, which is longer than Bridge to Gantry, in 9 minutes 57. That was back in 2013. Either people haven't been able or bothered to try and break it.

When I got the van back from the museum in February 2018, I had a few days to look around it and decided what I'd change; then Ed, from M Sport, a Transit specialist, wanted it for a load of dealer shows, so he had it for a month. Then, in early March, Ed took it straight to Cadwell where I was going to drive it while the TV lot filmed the beginning of what will become the Nürburgring van show.

I had Cadwell to myself, a private track day in the van. What a day! Still, the day before I was thinking, Why am I doing this when I'm so busy at work? I've got enough to do in my shed. I don't know what's up with me sometimes. Part of the problem was my lack of interest in this Trannie, but that wouldn't last. Once I'd done a load of changes it'd be a bit of me. It didn't take me long to realise what a lucky bastard I am, getting to razz this 700-horsepower Trannie round a deserted track.

The only real experience I'd had in the van, since it was fitted with the daft engine, was racing it at the Silver State Classic, and that was pretty much a straight flat-out race for 90 miles with a handful of corners along the way. Then I drove it on Bonneville Salt Flats, flat out in a straight line, trying, and failing, to break a land-speed record there. Both those places were about flat-out speed, acceleration and, in the case of Bonneville, traction, not handling. The van did eventually get up to 170mph on the roads of Nevada, but I was worried the wing mirrors would be scraping the floor going around corners on a race track.

I was sure it was going to be proper shit around a place like Cadwell, but I was impressed. It wasn't bad at all. The gearbox was terrible, but everything else was all right. The gearbox was out of the smaller of the Mustangs, the 3.7-litre one; it was a Getrag gearbox. The gearbox to have is a Tremec T-56, which Ford fit to the 5.0-litre Mustangs. Then you can get a sequential kit for them. Sequential gearshifts mean you change gear by pulling the lever back and forwards, not moving it through an H-pattern gate like a regular manual car. It makes gear changing very slightly quicker.

The main people who were involved in getting the van ready for the original Silver State programme were at Cadwell – Paul and Dan from Krazy Horse and James from Radical. The idea for the day was for me to take the Transit around the track, to get a measure of how good or bad it

Phil Read's Evo. 800 horsepower at Time Attack.

Supercharged Honda NSX, trick.

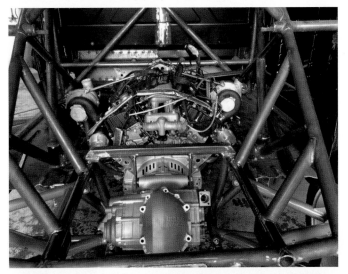

Work in progress for the Trannie at the Nürburgring. Hopefully by the time you read this it will have broken the record.

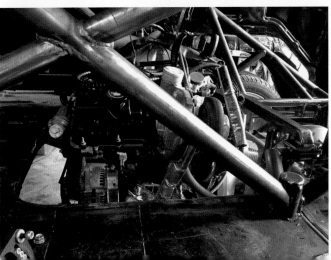

First time out on Les's
Rob North, work to do
... You can see the broken
dogs on the gear.

Trying out different power at JCB Headquarters.

Inside the Dakota DC12, that's the plan for the 75th anniversary of D Day.

The Avro Shackleton, came after the Lancaster but it's nothing like the Lancaster Bomber. It's got Rolls Royce Griffon engines and not Merlins and contra rotating propellers.

Shitting a brick.

British Grand Prix, Silverstone grid.
Swarmed out with knobbers ...
almost.

Ford DFV, most successful
Formula One engine ever.

In the Williams Grand
Prix museum,
Metro 6R4.

Krazy Horse chopper at
Dirtquake. Hard work
… good build.

Moriwaki RC30, rare as rocking
horse shit.

The boys having a day off.   The splinter group from Nigel Racing Corporation.

It is what it is, impressive.

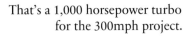

Bill Warner, he was the man. So I'm trying to start where he left off.

That's a 1,000 horsepower turbo for the 300mph project.

Turbo compound Hayabusa, they're pushing for the 300mph job too.

At Spa, met Joel I think … interesting bloke, small world.

was, then those involved would decide what happened from there.

They were all there, while the crew are filming, 'Yeah we can do this, we could do that.' Then someone came up with the idea to put an independent back axle in it, so the van would have independent suspension. At the moment it's got a live axle in it, which is the diff (that is the differential) and the axle all in one lump. By that I mean the diff is in the axle casing and the wheels bolt to the axle casing. It's not a very sophisticated set-up.

The diff that is currently fitted is shit; it's out of a Ford F-150 pickup, and this van, with all the power it has and the plans we have for it, could do with a limited slip diff. With a live axle, as soon as one of the back wheels goes light all the power goes to the wheel still in contact with the ground, because that's how a diff works. When that happens the whole van would go into a spin if you're not careful. Nearly all recent rear-wheel-drive cars have IRS (independent rear suspension), but American stuff doesn't usually. Live axles, like the Transit currently has, are good for drag racing, so maybe that's why the American manu-facturers stick with it. Performance on the quarter-mile drag strip is the traditional American way of selling speed, performance and fast cars to the masses.

While everyone's talking I'm not saying anything. They're all clever lads and that, but it was my idea to get the van out of the museum and do some work on it, and I think one of the biggest problems is I'm sat so high up. That means my mass is high so the vehicle's centre of gravity is higher. No one's mentioned that. Can't the seat be bolted directly to the floor of the van, so I'm virtually sitting on the floor and have a pedal box? We don't need more power, we don't need a lighter crank, or some of the other stuff they were talking about.

The reason I didn't say anything was because I'd already made my mind up that I'm going to do it all. I know that the next time I do a filming job I'll be asked when they can pick the van up to deliver it to Krazy Horse, or whoever, and perhaps I should take the path of least resistance, and let them, but I'm not going to. This van, and what I have planned for it, is down to me. I don't want it to be farmed out, just to make sure it's done to a timescale the TV lot have set. Uncle Rodders and his mate Tim Dray will help me out with it, but I want it to be done in my shed at home. The plan? I'm going to take the engine out and put it in the back, mid-engine it. Then it really will be a bit of me.

CHAPTER 18

'Back in my shed it was like *Crime Scene Investigation*'

AS YOU'LL HAVE already read, I was done with serious racing. Properly done this time, but I was spending as much, if not more, time in the shed working on bikes than I'd done for years.

Les Whiston, a Rob North specialist, had loaned me one of his Rob North BSA Triples to develop and race. The basis of the bike is the same as my dad's, the first proper race bike I'd ever ridden, and also the same basis as the Wall of Death record bike. I've been making a load of parts for it and I want to race it in Ireland and at CRMC, Classic Racing Motorcycle Club, races on short circuits.

I entered the classic class at the Cookstown 100, the start of the real road-racing season in Ireland, held at the end of April 2018, just outside the village of Cookstown in Co. Tyrone. The filming job in Russia and working long hours in the truck yard meant I ran out of time to be ready to get out to Cookstown, but I thought I could race at the CRMC's Snetterton round nearer to home in Norfolk. I'd much rather do a road race, but you've got to look at how much time you'd get on the bike. If I went to the Cookstown, I'd get half an hour of practice and a half-hour race, so it wasn't sensible. And not having to travel out to Ireland meant I'd have another couple of nights to get ready. I rang the CRMC's race entry secretary, Anji Yardley, to get an entry, and she was spot on. Then, at the eleventh hour, I couldn't get there either.

The problem causing the hold-up was the prototype gearbox that Les was developing. It's a cassette-style 'box, a much more modern design than the shit one these engines originally had, but it was taking a while to get all the bugs out of it. In the meantime, I couldn't even use a regular gearbox, because I'd altered my engine cases for this new style and couldn't go back without fitting a new engine, so we had to persevere with it.

We'd tried loads of stuff with the gearbox on the dyno, that's a rolling road that measures the power and torque. Then I was mucking about with it on Race Lane, a road out the back of work. I did maybe 20 to 30 miles up and down there. The gearbox was still far from perfect, but it was rideable and the only way to make it better was to keep riding it and changing a bit and riding it again.

The weekend after Snetterton was Tandragee, where I'd raced the Honda Superstocker in 2017 to get all my signatures for that year's TT. It's another Irish road race on a circuit I love. I'd had my Tandragee race entry in for ages, but as the date drew closer I realised it wasn't a sensible place to race a new, untested bike with a gearbox I wasn't 100 per cent sure about, so, again, I changed my mind at the eleventh hour. I was fairly confident in the bike by now, but I pulled out because it was all a bit unknown and Tandragee is not a track you want anything going wrong on. If you think the TT is short of places you'd want to crash, you want to see Tandragee. There was a track day at Cadwell Park in Louth that weekend and going there to test was the most sensible option. I'd get more time on the bike and, within reason, I could come in and out as I pleased.

Cammy and Trellis came with me, which was good. Cammy's my mechanic mate, and I've known Trellis – Johnny Ellis – since we were at school and we were apprentice truck fitters together at John Hebb Volvo. Trellis moved to Ireland to be my mechanic, in 2004, when I was racing for Robinson's Concrete. We both lived in an old Mercedes race truck at the concrete yard for a few months, me racing every weekend I could and both of us servicing their trucks in between.

The weather was brilliant when the three of us rolled into Cadwell's paddock. When it was time to get on track all the riders in my group did three laps behind the marshal's bike, as you have to do, then I did five laps before the gearbox grabbed two gears at once and the gearbox shit itself. The first thing I thought was I'm bloody pleased I wasn't at the Tandragree!

When it grabs two gears like that the gearbox locks up and the bike breaks the weakest link in the drivetrain. Normally the weakest link is the connection of the back wheel to the track, so the bike starts skidding and you've got a job on to control it, because pulling the clutch in doesn't make any difference. But, because I'd done a few laps, the track was dry and hot and the tyres were warm, it didn't break the friction and the back wheel kept turning, so something else had got to give to allow the bike to keep moving forward. The next weakest link was the teeth on the gears themselves, so it broke them, but I could keep rolling.

I managed to roll back to the pits at walking speed, the bike going, stuh-shom, tuh-gom, stuh-shom. Trellis said, 'Right, what are we doing? Getting it in bits to see what's up?' 'No, boys,' I told them, 'she's fucked.' I didn't need to look inside to know I wouldn't be riding it again that day.

It's only a half-hour drive home, so we got the bike back to my shed and drained the gearbox oil. It was mint, so I thought, Maybe I am wrong. Maybe it is something simple. I was expecting to see it pouring out like liquid metal, full of bits of broken gear teeth and shards of wreckage. Then we took the side casing off and realised that the oil was clean because all the bits of metal were so big they wouldn't come out of the drain hole.

Les races one the same and he'd had the same problem with the gearbox at Mallory Park. He thought the problem was a stretched circlip, used to retain part of the gearbox. He'd had his gearbox in and out that much, and hadn't put new circlips on every time like you're supposed to, and he reckoned one had jumped off and that's what allowed him to grab two gears.

Back in my shed it was like *Crime Scene Investigation* as the three of us tried to work out what had happened. All the circlips were in place, so it wasn't that. We saw that the shim washer had broken. A shim washer is a flat spacer, like a washer that goes under a nut or bolt, and is available in different thicknesses. Fitting the correct thickness allows you to space the gearbox accurately. This 3mm-thick shim washer had shattered, fallen out and allowed the gears to move and grab two together. It turns out the washer had gone through the wrong hardening process and had been through-hardened, not case-hardened. It was a perfect example of 50p part buggering the whole job.

I'd had a bit more luck racing a classic Suzuki Superbike. Peter Boast is a mate of mine who has raced everything for ever, set up the whole flat-track series in Britain, instructs on track days and runs his own flat-track school, on Tim Coles's family farm near Caenby Corner. I've known him for years and he asked if I wanted to do some Classic Endurance racing, the pair of us as teammates. I was well up for it.

The first time we raced as a team was a four-hour Classic Endurance race at Spa in Belgium. As a team we were, I suppose you'd say, the official Suzuki lot, Team Classic Suzuki. The bike looked like a Katana, but had a special frame. They had built it as a bit of a marketing exercise for the classic parts side of their business, assembling it at the Motorcycle Live, NEC bike show in November 2015. Nathan Colombi built it and did a hell of a job of it. He works with Steve Wheatman, the owner of Team Classic Suzuki Racing, restoring a lot of his Suzuki stuff.

Me, Shazza and my dad drove out to Spa in July 2017. We travelled out earlier in the week, so I could do a track day beforehand, on my Africa Twin road bike, to get an idea of where the track went. What a track.

On Friday morning we went to the Bastogne War Museum, in Belgium. The museum is quite new, only opening in 2014, and it focuses on the Second World War Battle of the Bulge, which took place in that region in the winter of 1944–5. It was the Germans' last big push and it caught the Allies by surprise. There's disagreement over the combined number of servicemen who died on both sides, but the smallest estimates are over 150,000. The battle began six months after D-Day, with the Germans trying to push forward to seize the docks at Antwerp, control the Western Front and then concentrate on the war with Russia on the Eastern Front, but the Allies won the battle and Germany never recovered. We were all well into the museum, and it was good to spend some time there away from the racetrack. Then in the afternoon we did qualifying ahead of the race on Saturday.

The qualifying for the Classic Endurance series is decided by both riders doing a session each and the average of their best two lap times decides where you start on the grid. You each have a 40-minute session, then you swap.

Classic Endurance racing is competitive, but it's nothing like Le Mans. We practised wheel changes and all that, though. There are some fast teams, like the Neate Honda team, a father and son team from Britain. Phase One, another British team and World Endurance champions on modern bikes, now race classics, too.

The Spa race started late in the day, so teams had to compete in daylight and in the dark. I'd been a bit quicker than

Boastie in practice, just two or three seconds a lap, but it was wet on race day and I was ten seconds a lap quicker. We were having a bit of bother with the lights after it got dark, then the race didn't go the full distance because someone chucked a load of oil down with half an hour to go and the track conditions, oil on water, were too dangerous to continue. We finished seventh, but we might have done better if it had gone the full four hours. I don't know for sure. Anything can happen in an endurance race.

That race was the best motorbike thing I did in 2017, but, saying that, the rest of the year didn't take much beating. Spa was some icing on a turd cake.

After Belgium I raced a Manx Norton at Goodwood Revival in September 2017, then nothing until the middle of May 2018, when I was back racing Classic Endurance, this time at Donington.

I rode 1980s Suzukis at both the Classic Endurance races, but with two different teams. In Belgium I was with the official Classic Suzuki team, then Boastie and his mate Pete, from B&B Motorcycles in Lincoln, came up with the idea of forming a different team, Team Lincs Classic Suzuki, for Donington. They did a lot of the organising, but the bike belonged to a mate of theirs, Ken from York. It was an XR69 replica, a Harris frame with a Suzuki 1200 Bandit engine in it. It takes a lot of folk to run an endurance team, with mechanics, foremen, chefs to feed everyone. Because classic racing attracts enthusiasts, a few blokes in the team own similar race bikes, so they know it well.

The official Team Classic Suzuki lot were racing at Donington, too, on the bike me and Boastie raced in Belgium, but they were our competition this time. They had John Reynolds, Steve Parrish and Michael Neeves riding for them.

John Reynolds – what a nice bloke – is a three-time British Superbike champion and was a privateer in GPs and a factory Suzuki World Superbike rider. He's 54 years old now, same as Boastie. Steve Parrish is always friendly when I meet him. In his day he was a very good racer, competed in grand prix, not a messer and still riding well at 65. Michael Neeves – not to be confused with my mates from Lincolnshire, the Neave twins – is one of *MCN*'s road testers. I don't really know him, but he seems an all right bloke.

In the European Classic Endurance series you can have two or three riders, but riders are in categories of gold, silver and bronze, depending on their results in National and World championship series since the year 2000, and you can't have two gold riders in the same team. A team can have a rider under 30 years of age, but he must be partnered with one of 45 or older. These handicaps are there to help the racing keep more of an amateur feel. I'm not under 30, and Boastie is over 50.

I hadn't ridden at Donington for years; the last time was

on the Smith's Triumph in 2015. For the Classic Endurance we raced on the short National configuration of the track, not the grand prix circuit with the Melbourne Loop. Practice and qualifying was on Saturday, warm-up and four-hour race on Sunday.

I hadn't ridden competitively for ten months, since the previous year's Spa Classic, and I'd never sat on this bike before, but I never have much bother swapping between bikes. All I've ridden this year, in the way of race bikes, is right-side, road-shift gear change, because that's what the Rob North BSA has, and I've hardly even ridden that. For this race I was jumping on the Suzuki that had left-side, race-shift. That means I'm changing with my right foot on the British bike and left with the Suzuki. And on the British bike I'm pressing down for first gear and up for the rest, where the Suzuki was up for first and down for the rest.

I couldn't get any clear track in qualifying and I think mine and Boastie's combined qualifying time put us 8th out of 55 bikes, but qualifying isn't crucial in a four-hour endurance race. The bikes line up on one side of the track, riders on the other, for the Le Mans-style start, then run over the track, jump on, start the bike and peel onto the track. The quickest qualifier is right on the start line and all the others are lined up alongside, at something like a 45-degree angle, front wheels pointing onto the track, of course.

I was asked to do an interview by the Suzuki people in front of the crowd. It was the husband of Anji Yardley, the helpful CRMC race secretary, asking the questions. 'So you're riding this XR69 . . .' he said, but I felt I had to put him straight and say, 'That's not an XR69. It's got a Suzuki Bandit engine in it. It's based on a GSX-R1100, that dates back to 1986, but they were making that engine right up to 2007. They're making 160 horsepower, running on, they're fitted with quickshifters, so it's not really being true to the sport in my mind. To me that bike should have an eight-valve GS-based engine with a roller-bearing crank. That was what an XR69 was.'

Plenty of teams are running the same specification, so it's not cheating, and this spec of bike is what's racing at the Classic TT. I'm not sure if they'll ask me for another live interview.

When we'd raced at Spa with Team Classic Suzuki, it was decided I'd do the first session, because I was the quicker of the two of us, meaning Boastie would have done the last session if the race had run its course. With the riders swapping every 40 minutes or so, Butch, the foreman of the Donington team, had a think about this and decided Boastie should start the race and me finish it. The European Classic Endurance series had gone to Aragon in Spain after Spa, but I couldn't race because Shazza was calving, so they had Boastie and Michael Neeves racing. Boastie went out on the last stint and slid off with four minutes of the four-hour race to go while he was on for a podium, and they wanted to avoid that playing on his mind.

Butch thought that if we were battling for a finish they wanted me on the bike when other riders in the race were tired and the field was a bit thinned out from crashes or breakdowns. I was happy either way. So Boastie did the running start, though neither of us are brilliant runners. Especially not in leathers and motorbike boots.

It seemed like a theme to the race bikes I was spending time on in the first few months of 2018, because the gearbox was terrible on this Suzuki, too. We both agreed it was bad. I moved the gear lever and thought it was a bit better, but Boastie didn't. It kept jumping out of gear when either of us shifted down the gearbox. It was just worn out, I think.

Boastie finished the first stint in eighth or ninth place, had the bike refuelled, then I jumped on and left the pit lane. Before the end of the lap I was thinking, This isn't safe. The bike wanted to jump into neutral every time you shifted down the 'box. If it jumped out when I was in a pack of bikes I had to run real wide to avoid everyone and stay out of their way while I got it back in gear. I had to compensate for it everywhere so it didn't make for good progress. I thought about parking it up, but kept at it, and was up to fifth or summat at the end of my forty-minute session. I'd worked out how to get around a lap only changing gear four times. I was going up one gear on the start/

finish straight, back one for Redgate; up one coming out of Redgate, then I'd hold third gear, all the way to the Chicane, before the start/finish.

If the gearbox was as good as it should've been, because Suzuki road bike gearboxes are normally good, I'd have been changing gear 12 times. I don't know of another race engine you could get away with two gears for a lap of Donington, but it had that much torque it was possible. Stewart Johnstone built the engine. He was the TAS engine builder when I was racing for them. The motor had done a bit of work since he built it. I can't imagine he'd build an engine with a worn gearbox, but the bike had done the Classic TT, what I still sometimes call by its old name, the Manx, and had six hours of work, all going well, during this weekend.

Team Classic Suzuki, Reynolds, Parrish and Neeves, were doing well, just in front of us, when their bike shit itself. I think it ran out of oil.

I'd stand and have a natter in between my sessions. Shazza and Dot came on the Sunday. Shazza had her phone out and could see the live timing so we knew how we were doing in the race. Then Butch would come into the awning to tell me when Boastie was coming in and when they wanted me in the pit lane ready to go.

Boastie was dead consistent, just plugging away. Early in the race he'd come in for the changeover in sixth or seventh, then I get on, go that little bit quicker and get us back to fifth or summat. I'd worked out a way of riding round the gearbox problem. I was still only using two gears, but I was holding my foot against the gear lever going into corners, so it would still jump out, but it would jump straight back in again. I couldn't be rushing about, but it did the job. I tried to explain to Boastie what I was doing in the few seconds as we swapped riders, but I don't think he got the gist.

We'd worked our way up to second, then dropped to third going into the final session. I'd told Butch that I didn't want loads of info on the pit board, just how many minutes to go and what position we were in. I don't want all that fist waving over the pit wall. I just want to concentrate and that's what I did, so we ended up coming second, behind a Dutch team on another Suzuki. The top Honda team, the Neates, crashed. Phase One crashed. To finish first, first you must finish, but that's easier said than done in endurance racing.

We had a barbecue afterwards, everyone helped pack the garage up, then I jumped in the van and headed home. It was a great day. I liked the challenge, though I didn't enjoy the riding as much as I would have if the gearbox had been better. Still, the whole experience was great. I like the whole team effort. I did leave thinking, What a great event, how good is it to be away from the modern stuff, but I'm glad I'm not doing this every weekend like I used to. Who gives a fuck? I can still put in an all right lap, but I don't need to

Rocester itself is a small village in Staffordshire, on the Derbyshire border, and the footprint of the JCB headquarters can't be much different from the size of the whole village. Just driving up to the place is impressive. In front of the massive grey steel building, with the famous yellow and black logo high on its wall, is a lake that the public can walk around; the grass is all perfectly cut and everything is spotless. Rocester is the place where Joseph Cyril Bamford began his company, in 1945, just at the end of the Second World War. The company has always been headquartered there, even though it's a household name around the world and the firm is still owned by the Bamford family.

J.C. Bamford grew up in engineering, but left the family business to start out on his own, in a shed with some basic welding equipment he bought for a few quid. Mr Bamford was what they'd call a workaholic today. He died in 2001 at the age of 84, but by then had already passed the business to his son. Mr JCB said the problem with his competitors was 'they get out of bed too late and go home from work too early'.

During the tank project I got to know a few folk at JCB and they said if I ever needed to borrow some of their kit all I had to do was give them a call. It didn't take me long to phone them up, because I wanted to get cracking with the small dirt track I had planned for the new house. I thought I'd better get in before they changed their mind. The land where I wanted to put it needed levelling out, so I asked for a loan of some heavy machinery and they were happy to help out.

I drive fork trucks all the time at work, so I've got a feel for what the knobs do, but I didn't have the tickets to operate the machinery they dropped off. Luckily the bloke who delivered them was ready for this and was qualified to assess me in my own yard and now I have tickets to operate a fork truck, roller, excavator and backhoe. I can drive them all for work if I need to.

When JCB asked if I would hand out some awards to its engineers at their annual ceremony I was happy to do it. The first date, in March 2018, was snowed off and I couldn't get out of Lincolnshire, but I could make it to the next date, in May. They'd always wanted to give me the grand tour, but I didn't have time when we were filming, so I spent the day of the award ceremony with them, and it was fascinating to find out how much they do.

JCB started out making farm trailers from military surplus materials that were dead cheap to buy at the end of the war. Just four years later, J.C. Bamford designed the Major Loader hydraulic kit, that meant regular British-made Fordson tractors could be modified to take shovels, bulldozer attachments and muck forks. Mr Bamford knew he was on to something and kept developing the idea until he came up with an excavator attachment for the back of a tractor. That would be the blueprint for the backhoe loader, a piece of machinery that the company became so synonymous with that when most people see one they don't know it's called a backhoe loader, they just think it's a JCB. The company's trade name has made it into the *Oxford English Dictionary* with the definition of 'A type of mechanical excavator with a shovel at the front and a digging arm at the rear'. Before that invention trenches for building, water and gas pipes and agriculture were dug by hand, with pick and shovel, but JCB properly revolutionised the job.

Plenty of other companies make their own version, but JCB has half the market share to itself. It's not all they do; they make 300 different products in ten factories across four continents. They are a big way of going.

I was taken to one of JCB's own quarries. It costs them £5 million a year to operate and they use it purely for proto-type testing; they don't directly earn a penny from it. They can burn 3,000 litres of diesel a day just testing prototypes and the competition. They have other manufacturers' stuff in so they can benchmark their own products against what else is on the market. The quarry is state of the art, with a helipad so that wealthy buyers from big construction companies from around the world can fly in for demonstrations of the latest machinery.

How much did they plough into our tank job? It must have been £200,000–£300,000. I didn't see the pro-gramme, but I'm told it didn't come across as a JCB advert. They're not in the business of making tanks. They have some military contracts, but that's it. I think they did it because they're a British company and they're proud of what our engineers achieved and wanted to be part of celebrating that. If it gave them a bit of marketing, then all well and good, but they were doing it for the right reason and went over and above to make the tank a reality.

Because JCB are family-owned and don't have shareholders or the stock market to answer to, they think about things differently. The quarry is one example, the JCB Academy is another. A few minutes from the headquarters, in the middle of Rocester, the academy is housed in an eighteenth-century mill and is a senior school and training centre for apprentices.

The academy opened in 2010 and takes high school-age lads and lasses from a 50-mile radius of Rocester. The aim is to get the schoolchildren used to working in industry, so they have a focus on engineering and science-related subjects, and their hours are nine to five.

Pupils can apply to go there as a regular high school from the age of 14, though they're lowering that soon. At the moment students have to start at another high school then move to the JCB Academy when they're old enough. They take 200 pupils per year and the school is hoping to expand so they can take kids for the whole of their time at high school.

There are three main groups that the incoming pupils can be put in. One group is those whose parents think it's a good idea for them to be there. Then there's a very small group where it's the kids themselves who have decided it was best for them; that's their direction in life. The final group is the pupils that other schools want rid of. They're disruptive, or troublemakers, and the academy will sometimes take them. One of the guides who was showing me around the school's workshops told the tale of a lad who turned up there a few years ago with a record of behavioural issues a foot thick, and now he's one of the top apprentices at JCB. The academy knows for a fact they've sorted some unruly kids and put them on a better path, by teaching them in a way that appeals to them and in a way the kids can see is going to help them in the future.

If I'd have had an opportunity to do that when I went to school I'd have ripped their arms off. I'd have lived in a ditch to attend a school like that.

School leavers can apply for apprenticeships at JCB, or other big companies in the area, including Rolls-Royce, Bentley and Network Rail, who also have a stake in the academy. I was shown around the workshops by a couple of JCB apprentices. It was an eye-opener. I didn't know there were still places like that, where they give an apprentice a drawing, and say they can use whatever machinery is in the workshop to make the part. The apprentices explained that the tutors see how different people go about the task and work out what each of them is best at, before they tell them, 'Well, this is what we thought was the right way to go about it, but if you've done it that way, then that might be better.' It was brilliant. They had a load of kit, including a load of milling machines like mine, and a welding workshop. They wanted for nothing, except more space.

I bought my first second-hand milling machine at the age of 19, from money I'd earned doing barrow jobs, work on the side. I was building race engines, for other riders, from that age, but if I'd been able to go to somewhere like the JCB Academy I'd have had a head start. The idea of it is not a million miles away from an idea me and Andy Spellman have been working on, to have a place in Lincolnshire where local lads and lasses can visit on school trips and learn about some of the trades and careers open to them. We want to open their eyes beyond working in a call centre or in a shop; not that there's owt wrong with those jobs, they're just not for everyone.

Martyn Molsom, one of JCB's chief engineers who I'd met through the tank project, was showing me around and we drove to each site in a Volkswagen XL1, the little £100,000 limited edition hybrid that does over 300 miles to the gallon. Like most, if not all, motor manufacturers, JCB are looking to the future of different fuel sources for their products. Loads of their stuff is diesel and, because so much of it works in cities, there's pressure to make greener options. Having the Volkswagen on test was a way of seeing how other companies solve similar problems.

JCB are pushing for electric. They've launched an electric mini-digger, but they haven't just taken the diesel engine and fuel tank out and put the electric motor and batteries in its place. No, they've looked at it in a whole different manner. It makes me think, Does an electric digger or backhoe loader need to look like a diesel one when it becomes electric? The counterweight and the driving position could change. They also spoke about how inefficient tracks were, there's that much drag with tracks, compared to wheels, so they're always looking for something that would work right when it is on wheels. I could've listened to them for hours.

At the headquarters they have a visitor centre, called The Story of JCB, a permanent £5 million exhibition. It's like a museum, but they don't like it being called that, and it's dead interesting too, with machinery from the entire history of the company, a full-size wireframe excavator made by the artist Benedict Radcliffe and a display about the armoured backhoe excavators they sell to the American military. It was explained that mines have gone off underneath these JCBs and the drivers have climbed out unscathed. The military-spec ones cost £250,000 for the regular version, and £350,000 for the armoured one fitted with bulletproof glass, and they've sold 1,000 to the US Army alone.

The company aren't afraid of showing they've earned a few quid out of the job, and there is a display of models of all the aircraft JCB have owned, going back to the 1960s. They have a fleet of private jets, not little ones either, and Sikorsky helicopters. They're planning to build a £60 million golf course near the World Headquarters, to bring the Masters there. I don't know a lot about golf, but even I know that's a big deal.

What must that company be worth? And they want me to hand out awards to their best engineers. JCB encourage all their staff to keep studying and gaining more qualifications, and this do, in their own plush auditorium, was a prize-giving, recognising the achievements of staff from the young, newly qualified designers right up to senior management level.

I was asked to hand out the awards and framed certificates, which I was happy to do, then there was a bit of a question and answer session. Some of JCB's headquarters' best folk are saying stuff like they're big fans, and they love the stuff I do, and it makes me feel a bit awkward. I don't know what it is they love. I'm just a wanker, so I can't see it myself. And it's not my upbringing that makes me like that. While my mum's worse than me, and she won't take any compliments, I reckon if my dad was praised he'd get a strut on. He loves all that. And I'm not saying there's anything wrong with that.

During the Q&A someone asked about tractors and I told them I had a John Deere. That changed the atmosphere in the room for a minute or two. JCB are on the edge of the tractor world, with the Fastrac, that they have been building since 1990. It was a whole new and very specific kind of tractor. It's not a 15-furrow tractor, like my John Deere; it's more of an agricultural hauler. It's the perfect thing for pulling a digestate spreader. And it's quick, for a tractor. Not many folk complain about being stuck behind a Fastrac on a country road. I do prefer to buy British if I can. I bought the Aston Martin, and it bit me on the arse, but I don't regret it. If JCB built the kind of tractor I need for the work I want it to do I'd definitely look into buying one, but they don't. Yet.

At the end of the presentation, after all the awards and all that had been done, one of the top brass introduced their new electric mini-digger, as it drove onto the stage, and let me have a go in it. Then the brightest lads and lasses wanted to talk to me. Again, I don't know why. I'm not even an engineer, I'm a mechanic. A fitter. I can do a bit of machining, but I'm not a toolmaker. When I see them I think I should've worked harder at school.

On the drive over to Staffordshire that morning I was in the same mindset I'd been in for most of the year: look how much I've got on at work, how much I've got on in the shed: do I need to be driving across the country and spending the day with JCB? No, not really, I realised, but I knew it was the right thing to do. And I'm glad I did. I had a brilliant day and felt better for doing it. I'd go as far as to say they're an amazing company.

CHAPTER 20

'Where would I have ever met Jenson Button? He doesn't come and empty the bins at the truck yard'

AFTER RUSSIA, THE next filming job I was involved with was finishing off the classic Williams F1 programme. There was still a lot to do. When I'd left for Moscow, the engine wasn't even in the car.

Before the break for Russia we'd been doing a load of stuff on the engineering side of things and watching the engine being dyno'd was a highlight. Formula One and top motorcycle racing teams know the safe operating limits of every component on their vehicles. So, for instance, if a crank has a competition life of 100 hours before being rebuilt or replaced, the team note down how many hours the car has run with that crank in it. Each crucial component has its own diary or database, updated at every test session or race. Obviously, if another component has twice the life, it doesn't need refreshing at the same time. Keeping good records is especially important when engines are being taken out of a certain chassis, put in another one then maybe back again. Over the 35 years since it raced, the exact history of how many hours this particular Cosworth DFV V8 motor had been run for were lost so it needed a racing engine specialist, like Judd Power, to check everything over in the engine. Williams did the same for the chassis, checking and double-checking everything.

When the engine was finished it was strapped to Judd's water-brake dyno. This is another kind of dyno to the one I describe later, in the chapter about my sheds. It does the same job as the rolling-road type I have at home, but Judd's water brake is designed to test engines out of vehicles. It's still measuring torque, and allowing laboratory-style testing, but it looked like it had come out of the Ark. It did the job, though, and was a dead interesting part of the whole job. The time on the dyno is another round of checks to make sure the engine is not going to shit itself.

The DFV engine made 520 horsepower on Judd's dyno. That's an output shaft figure. Power is lost through the gear and driveshafts, so it wouldn't measure 520bhp 'at the wheels' on my rolling-road dyno.

At this point I was back to filming two days a week, and working at the truck yard the other three or four, depending if they needed me in on a Saturday, which can be a busy day in the haulage world because a lot of maintenance is scheduled in.

The next day of filming we were at Williams, where I helped rebuild the gearbox and fit the engine in the car. We had another day at Williams, fitting the bodywork, doing all the finer detail bits, putting the wheels on, then doing the first start-up. The engine had run on the dyno, and all these boys know what they're doing, but there's always a bit of nervousness when it comes to starting something up for the first time, especially a car as historic as this one. Keke Rosberg won the Monte Carlo Grand Prix in it! And I was going to drive it, the next day in fact.

Williams chose Turweston airfield, a stone's throw from Silverstone racetrack, for my first go in the restored FW08C. It was a gentle test for the car, and somewhere I could concentrate on getting to grips with it in a straight line.

Karun Chandhok, the Williams test driver and F1 TV pundit, who'd been a mentor and expert in the filming so far, went out and did half a dozen lengths of the runway, then it was my turn.

I was driving straight up and down, getting a feel for the car, getting used to the gearbox, the sensation of speed. I'd already driven another single-seater at this point, the Formula Three at Pembrey, so having my head out of the car and seeing the two fat front wheels spinning and moving as I steered wasn't anything new to me.

The Williams gives a lot of feel through the suspension. I felt like I was an integral part of the car. The steering rack is set up so the wheel only needs half a turn from lock-to-lock. You're not having to pass it through your hands when you're doing U-turns, like you would in a normal road car. The feeling of the downforce was really noticeable. As fast as that Williams is, 500 horsepower, 500kg, it still doesn't have the brutal speed and ferociousness of my Volvo estate. Round a track, if I was in the Volvo I would not see which way this 35-year-old F1 car went. The Williams would win a standing start drag race, but if we got a bit of momentum into it, if we drove, side by side, up to 60mph then had a roll-on race in a straight line, my Volvo would eat it alive. The old F1 car wouldn't get its nose in front and probably wouldn't go over 170mph, where my Volvo will do 200mph.

Sitting in the old F1 car made me realise just how much has changed in the years since this car was competitive. The steering wheel is like something out of a Jaguar XJS, with green leather covering. The dashboard has just two dials on it and five big toggle switches either side of it. You change gear with your right hand, selecting gears and shifting through an H-pattern gate like a conventional car; it didn't even have a sequential box never mind paddle-shifts. Lots of things about driving a car like this are unfamiliar, but not everything.

The next opportunity I got to drive the car, and the first time on a proper race track, was back at Pembrey, the South Wales circuit where I'd tested the Formula Three Dallara Mercedes. And, like the previous time, the weather was terrible, pouring down all day.

The lads from the Williams Heritage team, who I'd got to know well by this point, were all there. They'd all been F1 mechanics at the cutting edge, before moving to the historic side: Bob, Steve and the foreman of the job, Dickie Stanford. Dickie had been Nigel Mansell's race mechanic, then Williams's chief mechanic and team manager.

The mechanics were busy preparing and checking the car while we had a team meeting. Dickie Stanford read out the rules and told us how it was all going to run: Karun's going to go out at this time, he'll do this many laps, he'll come in, stay in the car while we take the bodywork off, sit there for ten minutes, then go out and do five laps, then he'll come in and you'll do five laps.

When Karun drove the track it was obvious it had a lot of standing water on it. He wasn't hanging around, and I could hear it spinning up and see it moving under acceleration from 100 yards away. He drove back into the pits, the team gave it a once-over, to check that no hoses or anything were loose, then he did another session before it was my turn.

Before I put a foot in the car, one of the mechanics wiped the smooth soles of my driving boots clean, so I wasn't driving with slippery wet boots. It feels strange holding your feet up, like a show pony, to have another man clean the soles of your shoes, but it's about keeping the car in one piece, not pampering me.

I stalled when I first tried to leave the pit garage, and the car took a bit of starting after that. I think the engine was flooded because I hadn't kept the revs up, but it was no bother after that, and I didn't stall it again.

When I first went out I thought I was going to struggle to see because the water was covering my visor, but when I got up to speed it was blowing off so I could see where I was supposed to be going.

It was a private test day, just me on track. The car was fitted with Avon wets and the rears were throwing up massive plumes of water, eight or ten foot into the air.

I was treating the car very carefully. It was aquaplaning a little bit in the slower parts of the track, and though I wouldn't have gone around quicker in my Transit, I wouldn't have been far off the lap times I was doing in the old F1 car. I'm not sure what we learned that day and the team were already talking about fitting in another test day, at Thruxton, before I left for the long drive home.

By now, it had been confirmed how the programme would end, like a lot of TV programmes do, with a challenge to give the whole thing a point. I'm fascinated by the processes of building a replica of a First World War tank, or restoring a 1980s F1 car, but just rebuilding a historic vehicle isn't enough for TV, you need a deadline. And, because Williams had said they didn't want it racing in the FIA Masters Historic Formula One series, the compromise of me taking on Jenson Button had now been agreed. The 2009 F1 world champion would drive the Williams FW08B six-wheeler, a real oddball F1 car that showed brilliant performance in testing, but could never race because Formula One's governing body, the FIA, changed the rules, that effectively banned it before it could even make a competitive start.

The FW08B has four-wheel drive, and the rear four wheels are all powered. The FIA banned that. It has ground effect. The FIA banned that. And it had six wheels. The FIA said F1 cars could have a maximum of four wheels. That was it; the development hit a dead end, no way around it.

The TV lot managed, as they always seem to, to get everything arranged and the Thruxton test happened at the beginning of June. I'd finally get to drive the car in the dry. It was more time in the car, more time to get used to the gearbox and a few more laps to try and find out how hard

I could push the F1 car. I was allowed to do two sets of four laps of a circuit I know well, on an open practice day. Eight laps in total, because Williams didn't want to put many miles on the car; they just wanted me to have a feel for it in the dry. I drove home thinking, I'll be all right. I went ten seconds a lap faster in the second four-lap session than I did in the first session. I learned that the faster you go, the more committed you are and the better the car feels. You show it a bit of commitment and produce a bit of down-force for the air going over the wings. The next time I'd be in the car would be in five weeks' time, at Silverstone, for the handicap head-to-head race with Jenson Button. I thought I'd be laughing.

Our exhibition race took place on the Thursday of British Grand Prix weekend in July. I'd been filming the start of another programme the day before, the one about the history of the Dakota aircraft, but that's a story for another day. I'd been in Coventry, not far from Silverstone, and it would've made sense to stay in a hotel close to the track, but, if I can, I always prefer to drive home. That meant I was up at half four, as normal, to walk the dogs, have breakfast and leave at six. I'd made good time, I was early, but stopped for a cuppa, a few miles short of Silverstone, in the petrol station where I realised I needed to weaken the mixture. I only stopped for five minutes, but as soon as I turned off the A43 onto the road leading to the circuit, the traffic ground to a halt and I was late. Again.

The place was already rammed with folk, the campsites filling up with camper vans, ice-cream vans turning up, all the lasses that work in hospitality turning up, media signing on . . . Sarah, one of North One's assistant producers, was waiting for me with passes. We got a couple of bikes out of the back of the van and cycled into the circuit to meet Jenson Button and the team.

A few weeks before I'd been a guest at the Sheffield Doc Fest, a film festival that concentrates just on documentaries. I was asked by Channel 4 if I'd do a question and answer thing on stage with Suzi Perry. They don't ask much of me, so I said I would.

North One edited some clips together and Williams turned up with a modern F1 car. We did this hour-long thing onstage in the City Hall and I think it was a good do. There were two lasses onstage translating what we said into sign language and I reckon they had the hardest job of the night, trying to convert my ramblings and swearing into something that the hard of hearing could follow.

It was at the Sheffield do, a month or summat before the British Grand Prix, that it was announced I'd be racing Jenson Button. Up until that point only those involved with the programme knew the plan. Suzi Perry had asked if I'd ever met him. She wasn't the first to ask this – Ewan, the TV director, had when we were filming at Pembrey – but they both got the same answer: Where would I have ever met Jenson Button? He doesn't come and empty the bins at the truck yard. He doesn't work at the MOT station. Where would our paths have ever crossed?

While I haven't met Jenson Button, I have met Valentino Rossi, Nicky Hayden, Jorge Lorenzo, David Coulthard . . . Even though I keep myself to myself when I'm there, I've been to the Goodwood Festival of Speed where people like Jenson Button go. Telling Suzi Perry that there's no chance we'd have ever met is my way of trying to talk the job down. That's me doing my self-defence. There'll be some psychology behind it that I'm not clever enough to understand, but I know that's what I'm doing.

As part of the deal for North One being able to film at the F1 grand prix it had been agreed that me and Jenson Button would do a meet the fans thing onstage. A compere, a very official looking lassie in a Formula One shirt, was asking a few questions.

A hundred or so people turned up, the weather was perfect and there were lots of shirts off and beer bellies out. Jenson is obviously very good at that sort of thing, talking to the camera and the crowd, where I'm a bit of a knobber.

We weren't on track till after four in the afternoon, so I got a good chance to talk to Jenson. I was impressed with what a nice bloke he was. He's a year older than me, lives in California, does triathlons, so he's still a fit unit. He races a seriously fast Honda NSX in a Japanese Super GT series. It is nothing like a road-going NSX, but looks like one, and he was second in the championship when we met. We had a bit of pushbiking in common, so I asked if he'd heard of the RAM, the Ride Across America, or fancied doing it, and he had heard of it. He had also heard of the Tour Divide, or he said he had, but I noticed a look of vagueness when I mentioned it. He's an intelligent bloke, though, so perhaps he couldn't understand my accent.

I had a bit of time before anything else needed doing and I had wanted to go to Earls, the brake hose and oil line people who are based on a trading estate just outside the circuit, to get some hoses for the Nürburgring Transit, but I didn't really have enough time, so I sat in the café by myself and watched the world go by. We were in the top pit, where the Formula Three teams were set up. There were a lot of busy people, a lot of pink chinos and loafers with no socks and a lot of young drivers with their perfect hair, the right sunglasses and their shirts off. I've never been confident enough to walk around with my shirt off. Then it was back to filming.

We had both been asked to bring pushbikes with us and part of the day was the pair of us cycling around the track. Jenson was asking me a load of questions about motorbiking. He has a Ducati Panigale, a full-on Superbike for the road, and not very practical. I wondered where the enjoyment in riding one of them on the road was. I reckon you want a Triumph Tiger 800, mate, but I kept my mouth shut.

We had GoPros on the bikes, and he was giving me a bit of advice, telling me where the late apexes were and where he'd go down a gear, but he admitted he was only making educated guesses, because he'd never driven either of these cars.

We weren't swapping numbers and we are nothing alike, but I liked him. I respect what he's done and what he's still doing, by racing in Japan; it sounds like he was doing it for the love of racing.

After we did the lap on the bikes I had a word with Dickie Stanford, the team foreman. We spoke about how we were going to do this head-to-head. We couldn't call it a race, it was an exhibition. The plan he came up with was for both of us to be out on track together, have a rolling start, do three laps, then Jenson would come into the pits for 20 seconds while I stayed out, then for him to go back out and try to catch me up in the remaining three laps.

Before the head-to-head, we were given two laps to warm up. I've never driven, or ridden, Silverstone in the format we drove that day. Only F1 and MotoGP race it in that configuration. When British Superbikes race at Silverstone they miss some of the corners.

The six-wheeler Jenson drove is legendary among Formula One fans. It's like the one that got away. Imagine what F1 cars would look like now if the FIA hadn't put the anchors on the mad innovations of that era. But it is an ugly car.

Back at the Thruxton test day, I had met Frank Durney. Durney was one of Williams's designers in the FW08C and the six-wheeler era. He said he thought I might be better off in the car I was going to drive because people didn't know how to set up the ground-effect cars. It had given me a bit of hope that I'd have any kind of advantage over Jenson Button, a driver who'd spent 17 years racing in Formula One. I told Dickie Stanford this at Silverstone and he reckoned that even with its sideskirts removed the six-wheeler would have way more downforce than the Williams I was driving, so there was no way Jenson's car would be worse. That pissed on my bonfire.

We made our way onto the track for our two sighting laps. Jenson said I should follow him for the first, just to see the racing line for these kinds of car, then he'd said he was going to press on a bit to get a feel for the car. And that's what he did. He'd didn't fuck off, but he put a decent gap between us fair smartish.

The downforce of the six-wheeler was obvious straight away. As the car moves forward, air comes through front scoops, and is channelled under the car to a chamber to create a vacuum that sucks the car to the ground. Smoke was pouring off it down the straights. The ground-effect cars have skirts down the whole edge of the car, with Teflon sliders that rub on the track when the ground effect pulls the car down. The skirts seal the car to the tarmac, and, in turn, give the tyres more grip. The smoke is coming off the sliders and they leave black tramlines down the track.

The cars are loud and rattly. They're not as noisy as my BSA in full song, but they're loud enough.

After the two sighting laps we pulled into the pits and I didn't have any time to think about the circuit and what I could do to improve. Two laps isn't enough for me to get my eye in driving a car that's still quite unfamiliar on a track I don't know well. Perhaps it's long enough for a driver of Jenson Button's quality, but not for me. He was supposed to have a test in the six-wheeler at Thruxton, but he didn't turn up. He must have been confident. Before Silverstone, he'd never driven a Cosworth DFV-powered car before. Neither had he driven a six-wheel vehicle before, but he got in it, a car he'd never even seen before, and cleared off. I wasn't willing to push as hard as he was. He has so much more experience and feel for a car like this than I do.

Karun was there. He's very knowledgeable and, when he talks, I listen, but there wasn't a lot he could tell me that day.

It reminded me that the TV lot don't really understand how that sort of racing situation works. I can't be fast straight away. They thought: Turn up at Silverstone, have half an hour track time, we'll do a race of some sort or another, it'll be fine. But it's no good for me and the competitive nature I have.

Me and Jenson both sat in our cars, in the pit lane, for three or four minutes while the mechanics gave both cars a final once-over. Then it was time to go.

The last thing I was told before I went out was 'Don't crash it.' Saying that didn't do anyone any favours. I knew what the car meant to the history of Williams and all the folks involved. It didn't make me do anything any different, but it's a strange thing to hear before you're going out.

We set off again, out of the pits and towards the start/ finish line, at the back end of the circuit. We did a side-by-side rolling start. I was umming or aahing whether to be in second or third gear, but I left it in second and revved the nuts off the V8.

Jenson beat me into the first corner and I noticed how settled his car looked, drawn into the track both by the ground effect and, no doubt, his skill as a driver. I don't know how much slower the first of the non-ground-effect cars, like the one I was driving, compared to the ground-effect cars was per lap, but it did make a difference.

All that was going through my mind was, Don't crash it. I don't think anyone has ever said it to me before, and it didn't change the way I drove, but it was there, in my mind. My plan was to get on the back of Jenson in the hope he'd pull me along. If I could see where he was braking and turning then I'd shadow him as best I could. It only took one turn to realise he had so much more commitment into the corners and so much more corner speed than me. The reality slapped me around the face: he's one of the top 1 per cent of racing drivers in the world, he's won 15 F1 races, of course he's going to smoke me.

If I'd got straight out of the car at Thruxton and had got into it at Silverstone the next day, I would definitely have put up a bit more of a fight, and been closer at the finish; but driving a single-seater is not the sort of trade you can pick up just like that. I was still getting used to the lateral G. You don't get that with a motorbike. I did have a few slides and the car was pushing on, understeering, around a few corners, so I wasn't pussyfooting about. I was hard on the kerb on the way in and hard on the kerb on the way out in a few corners, which left me thinking I couldn't have done much more.

Rob Wilson instructed me in his technique of keeping the car level at Bruntingthorpe. That all went out of the window at Silverstone. Well, I say it went out of the window; it never even entered my head. There was too much going on. Like I said, it's not something you can pick up, it needs hours, days, of repetition so you're doing the things Rob Wilson teaches without thinking. I still had so much of the car to learn. I needed to master driving the Williams before I could apply advanced driving methods.

One of the trickiest things about learning to drive the FW08C fast is the six-speed gearbox, and how precise you have to be with the gear lever. When you're driving a car or van and you shift from second to third, you move the lever forward two inches, across two inches and forward another two inches before you select third. In the race car the movement was about a third the distance, so it was easy to select the wrong gear.

One time, when I was doing my best to keep sight of Jenson, I was trying to change from fifth to fourth, but I found second by mistake. I had a feeling I had it in the wrong gear, so I let the clutch out dead steadily. The rear wheels began to lock up, so I put it back into neutral. If I hadn't realised it was in second and I'd let the clutch out normally, it would've over-revved the motor and buggered it. That would have been as bad as crashing it. One missed gear like that loses you a couple of seconds or more and knocks your confidence in making a fast gear change the next time you have to shift down.

Jenson entered the pits at the end of his first half of the exhibition race and he was still in the pits when I drove by. I don't know when he came back onto the track, but he wasn't long catching me up. He said he'd showed me a wheel on the turn that leads onto the straight to warn me, but he knew I hadn't seen him, so he accounted for that, backed off there and got me on the brakes at the end of the back straight into the next turn. It would've been messy if he hadn't backed off and we'd come together on that corner.

This time, when he overtook me, I didn't take any notice of what he was doing. I just had to concentrate on how I was driving. And, compared to him, that was slowly.

It was noticeable that my tyres had gone off, because they were so soft. They're made by Avon, in Wiltshire, the only company that currently makes suitable tyres that'll fit these old cars, but Williams put big Goodyear stickers on the side, because that's what the car used originally and they want them to look authentic, with all the same branding as they had in the 1980s.

Jenson's car had four driving wheels at the back and two front wheels that steered. There were other six-wheel experimental F1 cars. The Tyrrell P34, from the mid-seventies, was designed with four small-diameter wheels at the front, that all steered, and two driven wheels at the back. Their idea was to lower the car's frontal area and improve aerodynamics. That thing won a Formula One race, in 1976, with Jody Scheckter driving.

Another British company, March, thought that improving the traction would make for quicker lap times, so they put four driven tyres at the back, but it never raced. Ferrari tried that configuration, too, and, again, never raced. Then came Williams, who proved the concept would work, in testing, before the whole six-wheel era was over.

After I saw the chequered flag I pulled into the pits and stayed sat in the car thinking about how I'd driven, trying to work out what I'd done. Jenson came over and had a natter and told me, 'You were shit into that bottom corner, you should've been later on the brakes,' which I knew. He was constructive in some other areas. There was no effort to blow smoke up my arse, and I appreciated that. We both knew I was shit.

And that was the last I saw of him. He had to go and do some filming. He'd be back to Silverstone every day because he commentates for one of the TV channels. He's dead good at it. I've got respect for him as a driver, no doubt, and also as a talker. I think one of the differences between me and someone like either Jenson Button or Suzi Perry is, if I've got no interest in a subject, I've got no interest in it and I can't turn it on and do a professional job of talking about it. I get the idea they both can. Mave, my mate who made *The Boat that Guy Built* programme with me, he could do that, too. I don't wish I could do it, like I wish I could drive an F1 car as fast as Jenson Button can, but I still respect it, because it's not easy and I recognise it as a skill.

When I took my helmet off I probably had a face like a smacked arse, because I felt I'd let the mechanics down, I'd let everyone down. I should have been beaming from ear to ear, after getting to race Jenson Button in Keke Rosberg's Monte Carlo F1-winning FW08C, but I got smoked, and I was disappointed.

I know if I'd have pushed any harder I reckon I'd have ended up in the barrier or in the gravel, not because I was on the car's limit, but because I was on the edge of my limits. I was understeering and getting slides, even though I was going slower than Jenson Button, because he would pick a different line, or have the car settled on its suspension better, or be balancing the throttle and brake differently – all those little things that make drivers like him the best in the world. It's the same way that he probably couldn't jump on a motorbike and stay with me around the Southern 100 course, even if I was on a bike I'd never sat on before. I knew my limits and I brought the car back safely.

I have a lot of confidence in my inner confidence: I do what I can do and I do no more. If I'd had another five laps, I'd have got quicker, and if I had another five laps, I'd have gone quicker again. But people don't get opportunities like this, to drive cars like the Williams FW08C on Silverstone during British Grand Prix weekend, so I'm not whinging. But I am disappointed I wasn't quicker.

The whole experience of being involved in rebuilding the car, meeting all the people – Steve, Bob and Dickie – was great. Probably the thing that stuck in my mind the most is spending a few hours with Dan at Judd, the company that checked, rebuilt and dyno'd the Cosworth DFV motor for Williams. I spent the day looking at all the oddball F1 engines they were working on, and at Judd's own engine, that is used in LMP2, the Le Mans Prototype series. The place was great, but Dan was, too. He's a bit older than me, and has two daughters who both race mini stock cars. I think they might use Mini engines, and the rules are dead tight so he'd bought an old water-brake dyno off eBay for £500 to fine-tune them. When I heard that I thought, That's ace. He was dead into it.

The whole experience was fun, and I like learning, so that part of it was good. I wasn't driving home in the Transit feeling like I had to have another go of that. I sound like a right ungrateful bastard, but what was I doing? Driving round seconds off Jenson Button's pace. Still, it was a great opportunity.

CHAPTER 21

'When it's blowing at full chat it feels like you're in a hurricane'

THE SHED, AND spending plenty of time in it, has always been important. Some of my earliest memories are of me sat on the end of the workbench quietly watching my dad prepare his race bikes before I was sent to bed. My first experience of hands-on engineering, in that same shed, was as a little lad fixing and tuning old petrol lawnmowers that people had chucked away. I've always spent a load of time in the shed and now that I'm not racing the roads so much I have more time to work on my own stuff, so I'm in my sheds even more. They're places I work on my projects, but they're also where I've earned an extra few quid tuning and rebuilding engines for other people.

Since I started writing these books I've lived in three different houses, all within ten miles of each other. When I started the autobiography I was living in my mate Dobby's house in Caistor. It was a big change in my life: I wasn't living in Kirmington any more and I wasn't working for my dad either, and Dobby's place didn't have a shed, but it wasn't far from my mum and dad's in Kirmo. Then I moved into another house and that had a decent-sized shed. It had room for my Volvo and machinery like the XYZ CNC milling machine I bought when I moved there. It had a 'clean' room that I used as an engine-building room. I was happy enough there until I found a half-wrecked farm with a bit of land. I won't lie: what appealed to me was that the knackered old buildings were more shed than house. The place needed rebuilding from the inside out, with interior floors, new gables and roofs, but it was all about the potential of those sheds. Now, a few years after I first saw it, the sheds are not far off being right.

The sheds are split into different areas. You always have shit in the corner of your shed. Stuff you don't use very often, but don't want to get rid of. I had shit taking over the place before I moved, so I have a shed just dedicated to putting all that stuff in and it's a fair size so it can store plenty of it. I've got the Pontiac in there, a Firebird that Uncle Rodders (who's not my real uncle) sold me when he realised he was never going to get the project he had in mind finished. This is going to be Dot's first car, if I have anything to do with it.

Next to the American V8 is the Mk3 Polo that Mad Adrian gave me after the engine shit itself. That's part of my back-up plan. I have a Land Rover Defender that we bought for Sharon, but she didn't get on with it. They've stopped making them now, so I thought I'd hang on to it to see if it goes up in value.

All the spare wheels for everything I own and all the spare tyres are in there. I get Morris oil in bulk, because I like treating all my vehicles to regular oil changes, and that's in there. There are loads of framed pictures, too. I don't have one picture hung in the house yet, so they're all waiting to be put up. There's loads of leftover building materials from when the house was being rebuilt: floorboards, roof tiles, toilets . . .

If I had to say what my number one shed was, it's the one with my main toolbox in. I've got a toolbox at work, but the one I have at home is called Mr Big (by Snap-on, not me). It's part of the KLA series, which has a deeper, longer construction, a proper heavy-duty thing. It's five or six metres long and above chest height, and I use some of the drawers and cupboards for storage of scales, battery chargers, pastes and glues, paperwork.

I bet I've spent close to £100,000 over the years on Snap-on, but the toolbox I have at home was the first thing I got from my Snap-on sponsorship. They don't normally do personal sponsorship deals (they support motorsport teams), but they have with me. I'm quite proud of that, pleased that they appreciate me as a mechanic and that they bent their sponsorship rules for me.

You can buy Snap-on on tick, paying off a bit every week out of your wages. That's how they get you. There's something you want, but don't really need, but you work out how much you can afford out of your mechanic's wages and talk yourself into it. Some mechanics and fitters don't care what tools they use, but the good ones want the best they can afford, and that, in my experience, is Snap-on. It's a good feeling to be working and knowing you have the right tool for the job. That's more than half the battle.

Also in shed number one, I've got my big eff-off lathe, the small lathe, surface grinder, parts washer, metal bender, plasma cutter, welder, porting tools . . .

The big lathe came out of a big factory in Grimsby, called Huntsman Tioxide. They shut down years ago and I bought some of the stuff out of there, but a long time after they'd closed. It needs wiring in and tidying up a bit.

The parts washer is something special. It's made by Snap-on, but it's not a UK-supplied unit, so it needed converting to 240V so it would run over here. It was part of one year's sponsorship deal, too. I'd have struggled to justify buying it myself, but I love it and I've used it loads since I've had it.

Nearly everything I'm working on engine-wise goes in it. It uses a very aggressive soluble substance in the water, so you have to rinse everything with clean water as soon as you get it out or you risk the components being corroded by the chemicals in the cleaner. You have to leave it on for half an hour beforehand to warm the water up. The parts come out of the washer cabinet bone dry, because it's heated. I've never seen an electric meter move so fast as when this parts washer is working. It's a thirsty bastard and a big unit, too. You could put a human in it. I could sit in it, but it wouldn't do me much good.

I've spent so much on tools because I love them and because I've doubled up on a lot of them I've got a lot of tools at home, and loads of very similar ones at work, too. The work tools are stored in a Snap-on Workstation. I've had it about 12 years and I traded in two smaller Snap-on toolboxes for it. When I say toolboxes, they're not something you pick up off the floor. They're metal chests with drawers of different depths. They're chin height and on wheels, or a bottom cabinet with a smaller set of toolbox drawers on top. The toolboxes I traded in were the ones I used when I worked at my dad's. Back then I'd pull my toolbox around the workshop so it was closer to where I was working at that particular time.

At Moody's, and the place I'm working now, you have a place of work and your toolbox stays there. That big bugger I've got now takes too much moving so that's not an option. It covers the floor area of a normal office desk but it's over head height. There's a load of storage drawers with a workbench on top and, above that, what they call a riser, which is an enclosed workspace with a lockable up-and-over door, like a car garage, on top. It's trick.

Snap-on tools are sold by agents who travel around their regions in vans. You can't buy Snap-on from Halfords or a DIY store. One of the most unusual things about these tools is the lifetime guarantee of most of them and the fact that the stuff is that good, that if you look after it you can trade in used kit against new stuff and there is a market for used toolboxes.

My milling machine, as I've said, is the XYZ CNC I've had for five or six years and have taught myself to use. The plasma cutter looks like a little MIG welder that has a hand torch with a button on it, but for cutting, not joining bits of metal. I cut sheet metal with it. I'll cut the bottom out of my Transit van with it when I get around to fitting the engine in the back.

I have a Kemppi TIG welding set. MIG is better for some things, if you just want to daub on some weld without concentrating the heat, but TIG is better for a nice, penetrative joint. TIG does titanium welding a lot easier than a MIG, too, if I ever get into that.

Also in this same shed I have all the bike stuff and a bike bench; a couple of good workbenches; a good air system, with air pipes plumbed round the workshop and take-off points positioned around the workshop to attach pneumatic air tools to, so I don't have a massive long air hose trailing behind me. There's my welding bench; a metal-working workbench and my other Snap-on toolbox – a tool wagon or TUV (tool utility vehicle) that's on wheels with big pneumatic tyres. It's designed for NASCAR pit lanes, and was part of the sponsorship, too. The partnership with Snap-on has been running for a few years so the stuff's added up. The tool wagon stores all my milling gear, so all the computer leads to link a laptop to the XYZ milling machine, all the cutting tips, cutting tools, boring bars, chocks and wedges, parallels . . .

Shed two is home to the vane compressor, which is rated at 20cfm. That means it pumps 20 cubic feet of air per minute, which is man enough for everything I need to run in my sheds and it's quiet because it's a vane, not a piston, compressor.

I have a Nissan GTR six-cylinder turbo engine out of a wrecked car that I bought off eBay. That's going in the Ford pickup project when I get my teeth into that. While I'm writing this, the Nissan engine is sat next to the Ford V6 turbo that was in the front of my black Trannie van, the one I raced at the Silver State Classic in 2016, but this engine is going to be bolted in the back of the same Trannie. I have a Scania 143 500 truck in there, too.

I have lifting legs for raising trucks off the ground to work underneath them and a two-poster car ramp, so I can service all my own vans and cars. Shed two stores a steam cleaner, another workbench and garden stuff like a chain-saw, lawnmower and strimmer.

The latest shed is my dyno room, dyno being short for dynamometer. I did a deal with the TV lot and they helped kit out the dyno shed. I have two Dynojet dynos. One is a four-wheel-drive car dyno that will measure up to 2,000 horsepower. The other is a motorbike dyno, a Dynojet 250i that will measure up to 1,000 horsepower. They both have Eddy current brakes, so you can hold the rpm at a steady state no matter what the throttle is doing. It's the same kind of brake a rollercoaster would have on it. A dyno with one of these fitted allows for a more accurate load test. If I was trying to get the fuelling right on an 800 horsepower Suzuki Hayabusa, the Eddy brake gives more controllable resistance, so the bike isn't revving out every time you touch the throttle. It allows you to see what all the sensors on the bike are reading while it's under load.

Like the parts washer, I'd got around not having my own dynos, but I had already used the motorbike one plenty of times in the first few weeks of owning it. The car one will come into its own when I crack on with the Transit and pickup projects. As with so many things, the more you use the dyno the better you get at it. I've already blown two bikes up on it, but that was nothing at all to do with operator error or the dyno.

I agreed to race the 2018 Spa Classic Endurance round again with Boastie. The lads who own the bikes that we race, Jez and Pete, and his mechanic Ben, had prepared some late 1980s GSX-R750s, the newest Suzukis the Classic Endurance series will allow people to race. They'd made a lovely job of these GSX-R750s. Both frames had been vapour-blasted, then Scotchbrited, to a really lovely finish. Scotchbrite is a bit like a kitchen scourer and is used to clean and finish metal. The engines had been rebuilt with loads of new parts including performance pistons and rings. We were hoping for good things from them, so they brought the pair of bikes down to set them up on my dyno.

In the case of the motorcycle dyno, the front wheel is rolled into a chock so that it's held securely. The back wheel is on a rolling drum sunk into the floor. The dyno operator, that's me, sits on the bike and operates it like riding a bike in a straight line. As the bike is started and begins to accelerate, it rolls the drum and the dyno system calculates the power and torque the bike is making.

I put the first of the Suzukis on the dyno and ran it up. Within a few seconds it had stopped running on all four cylinders and was only firing on two. I stopped the engine and we had a bit of a looking around, but we couldn't understand why it would stop. We took it off the dyno and put the other bike on. It did the same, but it stopped working even more quickly, if anything. When we moved that bike off the dyno, we noticed a load of fine, gritty sand where the bike had been running on the dyno.

We worked out that when the frames had been vapour-blasted, the medium that they put in the water to blast the alloy frames had found its way into all the nooks and crannies in the frame. As the bikes had been run up for the first time this dry, very fine grit was shaken loose. The bikes are never run in dusty conditions in the kinds of endurance races they compete in, so the air filters on the carbs are dead coarse. They're not designed to stop fine dirt, just bigger stones in case the bike slides off the track into a gravel trap during a race. If you do that with no filters on, the carbs can swallow stones and wreck the engine. Game over. When we took the filters off we saw the carbs were thick with this fine sand. It had got into the engines and buggered them. We couldn't believe how much of this grit had been left in the frame and what damage it had caused. It wasn't a good night, but we all learned a lesson, the hard way.

If I'm setting up a bike on the dyno, while I'm sat on it I'm looking at a laptop computer screen to see the power read-outs and the other information like air mixture. I can have one hand on the throttle, and one hand on the laptop adjusting the mapping of the ECU to adjust how much fuel is being fed in or the position of the ignition timing. There's more to it than that, but that's the basics. The dyno isn't just about measuring power, it's more about set-up and fine-tuning.

It's all right having a dyno that will measure 1,000 or 2,000 horsepower, but when you're kitting out your dyno room you have to do the calculations to make sure you can supply enough air to the engine to allow it to make that power. Turbos are sized in different ways. You have rotor sizes and input and output sizes, but, in general, turbos are referred to and rated by a number that is the maximum horsepower it can help provide. The turbo I'm fitting to the Hayabusa I'm building, the one I'm hoping to reach 300mph in a mile, is a 1,000-horsepower turbo. The bike won't make that power, because of the size of the engine, valves, intakes, loads of reasons, but that turbo will provide enough air for the right engine to make 1,000 horsepower. It's all down to the flow of compressed air the turbo can deliver to the engine.

These are rough figures, but to make 1,000 horsepower you've got to put 90,000 litres of air through that engine in one minute. That means, if you want an engine to make 1,000 horsepower for one minute, the turbo is taking 90,000 litres of air from the atmosphere and compressing it to mix with the petrol and be blown through the fuel injection system into the cylinder bores so it can be lit by the spark plugs. And when I say 90,000 litres, that's the air measured at barometric pressure – sea level. So, take a one-litre bottle and pour all the water out of it. What replaces the water in the bottle is a litre of air. Imagine 90,000 of those bottles. Every minute.

Turbocharged and supercharged engines can deal with this much air passing through their combustion chambers because the air is compressed and forcing multiple litres of air in the same volumetric area by upping the pressure it's held at. The more air the engine can flow, the more fuel you can mix with it, the bigger the bang when the spark ignites the fuel and air mix, and the more power the engine can make.

So, going back to my dyno room, it's equipped with one big fan that can deliver 500,000 litres of air per minute. When it's blowing at full chat it feels like you're in a hurricane. The tricky thing is keeping the room in a neutral state. It's all right getting all that air in, for the turbo to gulp up all it needs, but you've also got to get it out. If you don't, you're turbocharging the room, and your dyno will start reading mental numbers, because the turbo would be compressing air that is already being compressed by the room itself. That would never happen in nature. If you ran a non-turbocharged engine in a room that's not properly ventilated, it would behave like a turbocharged one. In most cases, when you're actually competing on a bike, the opposite is true. The higher you go above sea level the less dense the air becomes and a normally aspirated engine struggles to get enough in. That's why making good power at Bonneville, which is 4,200 feet above sea level, or near the top of Pikes Peak, 14,000 feet above sea level at the finish line, is more difficult.

That means you've got to get the air out so the atmosphere in the room remains at one bar, the air pressure at sea level. To do that I have a big, louvred grate in the wall. The air flows to it round two corners and the whole room is fitted out with sound-deadening panels and acoustic foam so the neighbours aren't too bothered by noise. The last thing I want to do is piss them off. That's why I don't run anything on the dyno past nine at night. The bloke who lives behind me plays drums in the shed at the bottom of his garden and I can hear it, and it doesn't bother me because he's good, so I think we'll be all right.

CHAPTER 22

'I stayed up the top end during the birth'

I COULD HAVE gone through life not being a dad and I'd have been all right about that, but, as of 23 October 2017, that situation changed for ever and I'm happy about it.

Dot, no middle name, was born in Grimsby. I stayed up the top end during the birth. The doctors ended up cutting her out of the sunroof. I didn't really want to see any of that.

Early on, like a lot of new dads, I imagine, I felt I couldn't do much with Dot. I would get home from work and talk to her about Nige and Steve. Just talking daft. I talk to her like I'm talking to another human being. I don't talk to her like people think you have to talk to babies. She seems a happy kid. She's always smiling. When I get up at four to take the dogs for a walk before work, Dot wakes up too, always looking like she is over the moon to have woken up to another day, smiling and full of beans at four in the morning.

I don't think anyone knows how they're going to react when they become a parent but, from my few months of experience, it's been good. I'll be honest and say it wasn't on my urgent to-do list, but it's made me realise as the job's evolved that now I can see I've got things I can pass on from my short time on earth. Maybe Dot will look at things differently to how I do, but share some of my perspective on life. There are pros and cons in everyone's personality, so hopefully she takes my pros and adds a few more of her own.

She is someone to leave my lathe and milling machine to. I didn't grow up with any of that. It was great having the shed, and the freedom to use whatever tools I could physically pick up, because I could build lawnmower engines, but I never had the chance to do any welding, turning or machining. I think if I would have had a lathe when I was six years old I'd be turning some good stuff out by now. I might have been a few fingers short of the full set, but I'd be a good machinist.

I keep telling people I would like Dot to be a welder, because women are supposed to make better welders than men. Shazza doesn't agree with my career plans. She says Dot will be whatever she wants to be. I'm the same, really. I want her to be a better welder than me, but she can do what she wants in life.

I'm a nappy changer. I get stuck in and do what little bit I can. I like it, but I have no idea how the job is going to go. There's no part of me thinking, She should be doing this by now, or comparing her to anyone else's kids. I'm taking every day as it comes. I just want her to grow up to be a good lass who can add a bit more to the world.

Sharon is the absolute best mum. She's brilliant. We have different views on good parenting, though. I think I might be rushing stuff. I bought a baby seat for the pushbike after a few weeks, and said I'd take her in the woods on the bike, but Sharon told me Dot's body wouldn't be ready for it until she's about nine months old. I'm not going to argue. As I said, Dot came to one of the Classic Endurance races with us when she was a few months old. Shazza organised some little ear defenders for her.

We had our first family holiday in June 2018. We had originally talked about driving to Italy, but it was too far to go with the young 'un. Then we thought about the south of France, but Shazza thought that would still be too long for Dot in the van. Eventually, we decided we'd stay in England and go to Monkey World Ape Rescue Centre in Dorset. Shazza is fascinated by monkeys.

We set off on Wednesday, dropping my BSA off at Les's near Dudley on the way down, so he could machine the cases to try to solve the gearbox problems we keep having.

We didn't have anything booked in advance. Instead, Sharon sorted hotels as we went along. The first hotel was a posh one in Christchurch; we ate in the hotel restaurant overlooking the harbour. We had nice hotels every night. The next night we stayed in the New Forest, another nice hotel. Dot was old enough to be put in a seat on a bike, so Shazza took her and I was on my bike, just having a steady pedal around.

We were going to get the ferry to the Isle of Wight, but there didn't look like there was much to do over there, so we went to Beaulieu instead. What a lovely place. It has the motor museum with Donald Campbell's land speed record-breaking *Bluebird* on display; there's a monorail to take you round the whole site and a country house. Beaulieu was dead quiet, because we went midweek, out of school holidays.

Along with the regular motor museum exhibits there is a *Top Gear* museum with a load of props and cars that have been used, and wrecked, in the making of the programme. It might have started tongues wagging if I'd been spotted in there because it was the same week that Matt LeBlanc had announced he was packing in presenting *Top Gear*. People keep suggesting my name as a replacement, but what reason would I have for doing that? I'm sure the presenters get to do some good stuff, but I get to do amazing things anyway. The museum showed a 15-minute film highlighting the best bits of the programme a few times a day and we sat down to watch it. It was just long enough to make me realise it was all utter bullshit. Entertaining, but pointless bullshit. There's no arguing it's a very popular show, but it's not for me.

The week we chose to go away was Isle of Man TT race week and, because Shazza's right into bikes, we watched some of the highlights on the telly in our hotel.

Michael Dunlop won the first Superbike and Peter Hickman won the Senior, setting a new lap record. I like Michael Dunlop. He's obviously a very talented rider, but what I noticed, and liked the most, was that Dunlop finished fourth in the Senior. I look at Peter Hickman, who, in my opinion, is a better motorbike rider of the two, and is the best of the riders out there. He can do it in the British championship and on the roads. There are a lot of very good motorbike racers but they don't have the balls for the road races. Hickman has and he's managed to race at the TT in what I'd say is the right way – he's built up to it in a sustainable way. That's why I'd say he's the better motor-bike rider. That's not saying Dunlop isn't a brilliant road racer. Just look at his results; he's one of the best ever and he has balls, but Hickman looks like he has more pure skill. To me, at least.

What impressed me about Dunlop in the Senior was he went out and didn't look like he'd ride until he killed himself. He rode to fourth position and he's lived to tell the tale. Tomorrow's another day. It showed a maturity that some people thought he didn't have in him. I'm sure he'll think about what happened, come back and smoke them.

After I got back off holiday someone told me that Dean Harrison was leading and broke down, then was leading another race and lost by a few seconds. They asked if his TT week reminded me of any of mine, and it hadn't occurred to me for one moment. It never even crossed my mind. One thing that did, during watching any of it, was the strong feeling that I was happy to be out of that world. I was so glad that I wasn't riding motorbikes around the same piece of tarmac I've been riding for ten years or twelve years, or however long it was.

I'm still thankful I got out in one piece. The TT has a bit of draw, there's no denying that, otherwise I wouldn't have gone back with Honda in 2017, after I was sure I was done with it. I walked away when plenty haven't. Another two riders died at the TT in May 2018, including Dan Kneen. The thirty-year-old Manxman died after crashing in practice on a Superbike. He was racing for TAS on the BMW Superbike.

I don't mean to be disrespectful to the TT, but I don't give two fucks about it now. It's a chapter of my life that's over. What reason is there for me to go back again? What have I got to prove? People still ask me why I don't go back, and when they do they're just showing a complete lack of understanding of the motivations involved in competing at a place like that. Going back because it's what I did and I was sort of all right at it is not a good reason to race the TT. It's not even a reason, never mind a good one. But I look at some riders and it seems that that is exactly why they do keep going back. They're not going back to win.

The years I raced there might define me to some people, but it's not what defines me to myself and it hasn't for years. Give me a day at Monkey World with Dot and Sharon instead.

If it hadn't been for Shazza I wouldn't have even turned the telly on. I was thinking, The Tour Divide starts tonight! When it did start I was straight on the trackleaders.com website to watch the progress of the leaders. Everyone competing in the race carries a SPOT Tracker, a little GPS device that sends a signal to a satellite so it can be traced. The website puts everyone's progress on the map so you can click on it to see who is where. 'Dot Spotters', that's what they call people like me who follow the race on the internet.

We were only away three nights. Sharon would have liked to have stayed away for longer, but I had to explain that she should be happy with what she'd got, not what she hadn't. We've had four days away: be happy.

If it had been up to me I would have gone to work or spent the time in the shed, but we've got a nipper now and I'll admit I only went away because I felt it was the right thing to do, but then I really enjoyed it. I switched my brain off from work and the shed. I can't have a week off at home because I can't stay out of the shed.

When I've been on holiday before I've always been itching to get back home, but I wasn't this time, so it made me think we'll have a few more days away later this year. We will go to France or Italy, when Dot's a bit older. I spoke to Gary, one of the MOT testers where we take the trucks, and he told me he'd taken his daughter to the Museum of Science and Industry in Manchester. That made me think there'll be loads of places that I'd like to go, that I would never visit off my own back, but it will be great to take Dot.

'Nigel Racing Corporation'

NIGEL RACING CORPORATION

THE NRC STORY starts with me driving out to the Monteblanco test, in Spain, where I rode the Honda Fireblade SP2 for the first time at the team's opening test of the 2017 season. As usual, Honda arranged a team get-together before the first test. Neil Tuxworth and Jonny Twelvetrees were there, so were the boys from the endurance racing team and my road-racing teammate, John McGuinness . . .

The idea of having a meeting like this gets all the introductions out of the way, so you're not doing so much of that on the first day of testing, when there's plenty to do.

I had something on my mind that I wanted to get out in the open. When I'm in a daft mood me and Sharon would come up with stories about our dog Nigel having a secret life. I'd started saying he was the founder of Honda's racing department and it always should've been called NRC, Nigel Racing Corporation, not what it actually is, HRC – Honda Racing Corporation. I'd told Andy Spellman about it, too, just spouting nonsense, and we even had HRC's famous logo changed to read NRC.

I reckoned this team meeting was the perfect time to bring up the story and let Honda know I was thinking of making some stuff with NRC's new logo on it. As we were sat around the table I started to explain, 'You'll never guess, that dog of mine only reckons he was the founder of Honda Racing Corporation and he's going to make some hats with Nigel Racing Corporation on them.'

I was talking utter shite for my own amusement, pretending my Labrador was the founder of HRC. It wasn't a conversation, it was a monologue. I was doing the talking and Honda Racing's top brass didn't say a word. This was the first time I'd met Jonny Twelvetrees, the 31-year-old team manager who'd been brought in to take over from Tuxworth, and I could see he was eyeing me a bit sideways, with a look on his face I read to say, 'He's bloody mental.'

When I said my piece Tuxworth was straight onto the next topic of conversation, talking about brake pads or something else irrelevant.

A couple of weeks later I was at Mablethorpe beach races, where Tuxworth nearly always goes because he's on the committee. I had the first prototype of the Nigel Racing Corporation woolly hats and gave him it, saying: 'Nigel's only gone and done it. Bloody stupid hound.'

The next time I saw Jonny Twelvetrees I gave him one of the hats, saying the same thing, 'Look what that dog of mine has gone and done.' They didn't know how to take it, but they didn't say owt. Again, it was for my own amusement. It wasn't taking my focus off the job in hand. I was riding that Fireblade at every test and race possible, even after seeing what it had done to McGuinness, and proving, at Elvington, that it didn't have the top speed to be competitive. I was still riding it as hard as I could in the circumstances. You've already read that the Honda job didn't go according to plan, but I was still putting my arse on the line for Honda at dangerous races, so I didn't feel bad about this bit of daft fun.

At the TT I had an NRC sticker on the front of my helmet, rubbing their noses in the joke a bit. I got the feeling that Tuxworth found it funny, but he didn't say anything or give me any clues. Remember, Jonny Twelvetrees had been brought in to manage the job by that stage, Tuxworth just overseeing things. Twelvetrees couldn't have one of his riders – his only rider because the other one had been fucked over by Honda electrics – riding around with a sticker that was a pisstake parody of the company's highly respected racing department. Then it became clear he didn't want to tell me himself, so one of the youngest mechanics came up to me and said, 'You've got to take that sticker off your helmet.' We were having a hard time as a team by that stage, we didn't need any more friction, so I put another sticker on to cover it up.

And that leads to the next part of the NRC story ... Take the broken backs and the singed eyebrows out of it, and racing has been bloody good to me over the years. I began racing motorbikes before I had my own car or van to get to the circuits, and I'd convince my mum to drive me to the races, where she'd read a magazine while I was preparing for the next session. I started out paying my own way, with help from my dad, spending all my wages from my full-time truck job and working a night job in Chicago Rock Café, collecting glasses, to earn extra to pay for the job. It was like that right up until after I'd competed in my first ever Irish road race, at Kells. I'd been spotted by Sam Finlay, who ran a privateer team, and he asked if I wanted to race for his Team Racing outfit. That was a big change in my life, and I moved out to Ireland, living in a half-finished bungalow, the Fungalow. That was the first step towards racing for different teams up until the end of 2017, when I decided to pack in that side of racing for good.

I felt I wanted to give a bit back, so I've been helping a couple of local lads, twin brothers Tim and Tom Neave. I've known them for years, and I'm good friends with their uncle, also called Tim. I've built and tuned their engines, and bought them tyres, right back to when they raced in flat-track. A few years ago, they both decided to pack in dirt tracking and start road racing. Now they're in the national championship, both competing in different British Superbike support classes.

Tom seemed to take to road racing better initially, but he had a shoulder injury, and needed an operation, so he didn't race in the first half of 2018.

I didn't really want it to be known that I was sponsoring them, so I've had them both agree that they won't mention my name. Instead, Tim says he's racing for the Nigel Racing Corporation and Tom is racing for a splinter group, called Stevowaki – another racing organisation with Steve, another of my dogs, in charge.

Nigel is four years old, and a big part of my life. We ended up getting Steve by chance, through a mate called Steve Broadbent in the Isle of Man. He used to work for the Steam Packet ferry, but now he sells anchors for offshore windfarms and oil rigs.

He deals with a lass who breeds Labradors. I asked him to let us know if they were having another litter. A while later he rang us saying, 'She's got one left, do you want it?' I thought it would suit Nige to have a mate, but my sister reckoned we didn't need another dog, and that Nigel was great by himself. When I spoke to people with dog experience they said two dogs is easier than one dog. It's all right me wanting one, so I asked Shazza, and she was happy to have another dog, so we ended up with Steve and he's been bloody brilliant. He's a better pup than Nige was, and he's a better dog now. Nige is very Nigel – it's his way or no way – where Steve is a proper pet. You give him a bollocking and he won't do it again. Nige is obviously the best, but he's a pain in the arse.

I like human names for dogs and Sharon is a big fan of Stephen Fry, so he's Steve. I think Graham is going to be the next one. And a goat called Ferris. And some chickens. I reckon if the goat grows up with dogs it'll think it is a dog. It won't be named after Ferris Bueller, but the one with the big dick in the film *Sex Lives of the Potato Men*. Ferris! You had to be there.

Steve is a bit of a rebel without a cause, Nigel is more calculating. Nigel is a better team owner, but Steve is a better dog. Nigel is always trying to kill Steve. He did it again last week. I let them out in the yard and they're no bother. Nigel will jump over the fence and clear off for half an hour, then come back, jump over the fence again and that's it: you never have to worry about him.

Steve can't work out how to jump over the fence. He has watched Nige do it every day and he's never tried it himself, but if the gate is ever left open, and Steve can follow Nige out, then they bugger off together. Nigel goes far enough away that Steve has no chance of finding his way back, then Nigel gives him the slip and comes back on his own. I once had to drive five miles to find Steve.

I get the feeling that Nigel's always planning: If I do this, that will happen, if I do that, this will happen. Steve is just 'Hiya! Huh, huh, huh . . .'

Nige took Steve right to the main road. I can imagine him saying, 'Steven, what do you think would happen if we walked into the road?'

Nigel is my first boy and I'd do anything for the pair of them, but there are times when I'm at the end of my tether with Nige. He came back without Steve again and he knew what he'd done. I could see it in his face. I threatened him with a long-term move to my sister's, but that's not really a punishment. She thinks as much of him as I do.

When they both escape Sharon goes mental with me (because it's normally me that's left the gate open). It annoys me that the dogs have buggered off, but what annoys me more is they've landed me in trouble with Sharon. When I find them I remind them, in the bluntest terms possible, they're a pair of bastards, and that I'm getting my ear chewed off because of them.

Anyway, both dogs have these race teams. Nigel's name is on Tim's Yamaha R6. If you're racing in the Supersport class, you've got to have a Yamaha R6. It's the only new bike out there really. The other manufacturers have stopped developing Supersport 600 bikes because sales of those kinds of road bikes completely died.

Tom competes in the Superstock 1000 class, where you have more choice. BMW, Kawasaki and Suzuki all make good Superstock bikes. I wouldn't choose a Honda or a Yamaha this year, so I bought a Suzuki GSX-R1000 for Tom. The lads buy the rest of the stuff they need: exhaust, spare wheels, race bodywork, clip-ons . . .

They used to race in the same class and it always had the potential to get messy, because they were so focused on each other. It's better that they're at the same race meeting, but not in the same class. One isn't looking what the other is doing and just trying to beat him rather than seeing the bigger picture and the other 20-odd other bikes out there with them.

Having the dyno in the shed at home has meant I could do a bit more than usual, especially with Tim's 600. The bike came with a World Supersport specification electronic control system. Neither of us thought it was that good and Tim said the bike was hard to ride with it on. Then the engine blew and I thought it was the fault of the ignition, detonating a piston through timing. I couldn't find exactly what it was, but we had been struggling with cylinder trimming, perfecting the timing and fuelling for each of the engine's four cylinders. We knew it was running lean on one cylinder, the one that shit itself. We had all the fuel injectors checked and knew there was nothing adrift mechanically. It was all perfect, so the only thing it could be was the ignition lighting the fuel earlier, or we weren't putting enough fuel in that one cylinder.

Tim bit the bullet and bought a 'kit' ignition system for £1,600 to solve the problem. 'Kit' means it's Yamaha's official racing ignition. It's not the most sophisticated, but it should be good enough. If you compare the kit to a MoTeC system, like I've used on Superbikes and Supersport bikes, the MoTeC is £3,000 just for the loom, £3,000 for the ECU and £1,500 for the dash, and it won't work without all three of them. With the kit system you can use the standard Yamaha dash and loom with the £1,600 ECU. The downside is the kit ECU doesn't have the same potential to help make as much horsepower as the MoTeC. And in the Supersport 600 class, where the bikes aren't making a massive amount of power, every increase you can squeeze out of the engine makes a big difference.

I was still learning the dyno when we plugged in the new ignition. Tim was under pressure; I had to go to work and I felt the fuelling was miles out. I made it safe on the dyno, but not that quick. Then he did a track day at Knockhill, where his next race was, and said it was loads better.

I don't go and watch either of them racing. I let them get on with it and wait to hear how they did. I'm not that interested in their results, that's not why I'm helping them.

Even before the season started I could imagine Tom getting on a podium, on the 1000, or even winning a British championship race in the near future, and not long after coming back from injury he did put it on the podium.

If I were being blunt, I'd say that, as good as they are, I'm not sure either of them is good enough to get to the point where someone is paying them to ride. There are hundreds of young riders out there all hoping to get picked up by a team, but only a handful get signed. I hope they prove me wrong, and, obviously, I'd be dead happy if that happened, but I'm not putting my money into the job because I think they're going to be the next Mick Doohan. I'm doing it because I like them. Like I said, racing has been good to me and this is my way of giving a bit back.

CHAPTER 24

'An entertainer, a showman. That's the last thing I am'

WHILE I WAS getting ready to write the final chapter of this book, I hadn't raced on the roads for over a year, but it has been on my mind a lot lately and, unfortunately, for the wrong reasons.

Road racing formed a big part of the early bit of this book, but it's well and truly over now. I look back (for what good that ever does) and think I should have done one year with TAS, in 2011, and called it a draw after that. The first year on the Suzuki was good, then I was just going through the motions.

You see some boys cross the finish line and they're going bloody berserk, jumping up and down and doing burn-outs. I've won a load of races and the moment I crossed the line, the feeling was, 'Huh, that's all right. What's on at work in the morning?' I might have put my thumb up, or a hand in the air, but the feeling of winning never took over me like it obviously does for some lads. I don't know if those riders are doing it out of excitement, or because they think that's what you're supposed to do, or they're trying to entertain the crowd, but I'm not an enter-tainer. Ken Fox, the man who taught me to ride the Wall of Death, is an entertainer, a showman. That's the last thing I am.

Even though I struggle to admit ever enjoying racing for teams, road racing still drew me back in. I couldn't resist the chance of racing the HRC Fireblade and riding the Honda Six. Luckily, I lived to tell the tale, getting away with it by the skin of my teeth. I knew, while I was walking back up the road to the Honda that had just chucked me off at the 2017 TT, that was me done. Fuck you all, I'm not coming back. That's not supposed to sound ungrateful, it's just what it took to break the spell and how I felt in that moment.

There was a bit of an interview with Neil Tuxworth, the man who convinced me to race for Honda, in *Performance Bikes* in middle of 2018. The magazine asked him about me and he said my mind must have been elsewhere and that's why the Honda did nothing in 2017 when I was on it. Mates asked if I was annoyed, but I wasn't at all. I like the man and he can say what he wants. He's Mr Honda Racing and he's playing the game. He has to pass the buck for the bike's poor showing, and if he passes it to me, that's all right. I don't have a problem with Tuxworth, and he's been round to ours for his tea since the magazine came out. I couldn't care less what he said, because I know the business and how it has to be.

People who look at the results that Fireblade had in 2018 will see I didn't have to say anything more. Those that know know, and now you've read this book, you know, too. If some people think I wasn't quick enough that's fair enough; just look what else it did the following season. And people were hardly bursting down the door to ride it.

The reason road racing was on my mind as I wrote this final chapter was because of a couple of fatal accidents involving people I knew well.

William Dunlop seemed to be on the verge of giving over, but he kept on going and on 7 July 2018 he crashed and died at Skerries, a big race on the coast not far from Dublin.

He hadn't had the best season and he missed the TT, so he might have felt pressure going into the race at Skerries. I felt there was a lot of external pressure on him to keep racing because he was a Dunlop. I always thought he had a similar attitude to me; he wasn't that bothered about the results, he just loved his riding. I was a teammate with him for a year, and he was a lazy bugger, but there was more to him than motorbikes.

The story I heard was a heavy landing knocked the sump plug out of the bottom of the engine and spat oil all over the back wheel. It's such a shame because he'd not long had a kid and had another on the way. Perhaps he was a victim of his surname. He was a Dunlop and Dunlops keep racing.

Just one week later, a mate of mine, another Lincolnshire rider, Ivan Lintin, just about survived a big crash at Stadium Corner at the Southern 100 on the Isle of Man, the race I loved attending most of all. Ivor Biggun is my nickname for him and he used to come to races with me, before he started racing himself. He's won TTs in the Supertwin class, and he was still a good goer.

From what I've heard, James Cowton crashed first and was killed. He was 25, from over the Humber from me in East Yorkshire. I didn't know him very well, but he was a very confident lad, a good rider. It sounds like Ivan couldn't avoid the wreckage and he crashed and was seriously injured, then another couple of lads crashed into the wreckage on the scene and broke a load of bones between them.

As I'm writing this, in August 2018, I'm planning to visit Ivan in hospital. I'm told he's opened his eyes, but I don't know what's going to happen to him, or what recovery he can expect.

When I saw Ivan or heard his name mentioned I never thought that he should pack in racing or that he was pushing his luck. I'd had those thoughts about McGuinness, Hutchy and Ryan Farquhar, but not Ivan. He's in his early thirties, a bit younger than me. He'd had the odd crash, like all racers do, but he wasn't a crasher.

Thinking about the accident made me grateful that in all my high-speed crashes, and there have been a few, I'd never caused anyone behind to crash. I've made some stupid mistakes and if someone had been killed on my wreckage it would be hard to live with myself. I would, of course, because I wouldn't have a choice, but it's a hell of thing to have hanging over you. Luckily, I hadn't had to deal with that. I've taken boys out, braking into slow corners, when I was new to road racing and a bit keen, but it was slow stuff and no one got hurt. I put a very dodgy move on Michael Rutter at the North West 200, at Mather's Cross, before they put a chicane in, and I found him after the race to apologise for riding like a wanker. He just shook his head, and I learned from it.

When I was in the thick of racing and would hear about the death of a rider, I'd think, That's another one dead, and forget about it. As heartless as that sounds, it's what I did.

Back in 2004 I went to the funeral of Tommy Clucas, a road racer I'd met a few times, who died at the Manx Grand Prix. I went with Martin Finnegan and a whole lot of other road racers. I hadn't been road racing long, but I sat there knowing I'd never go to another racer's funeral, no matter how well I knew them, and I never have done. I didn't need that kind of reminder of the risks. I didn't even go to Martin Finnegan's funeral, after his crash at Tandragee, and he was as a close a friend as I had in racing.

Riders who I knew to pass the time of day with would die at the TT or in Ireland and I'd erase them from my mind. I wouldn't even remember their names. The human brain is quite good at blocking things out, but now I'm on the outside of it, all I can think is how bloody dangerous it is.

In motorcycle road racing, your life is in the hands of other people – the riders around you; the marshals who might not have spotted oil on the track; the mechanics who spanner your bike; the mechanics who worked on the bike you're chasing up the track – and the margin for error is so small on those tracks. I remember, in 2013 or 2014, at the TT, the front-wheel spindle nut came off my Suzuki Superstock 1000cc race bike. A spectator saw it and told one of the marshals who waved me to stop. I righted it in my head that the forks had bottomed out and that had caused the nut to come loose, because I trusted the bloke who'd worked on my bike and he told me he'd tightened it.

All that trust and ignoring of the risks are ways of coping with things just so you'll turn up to the next race. Now I think I must have been mental. What was I doing? It's crackers and I wouldn't do it for all the tea in China.

When the mood takes me, I'm still planning to race the same Irish and Manx roads on my Rob North BSA, but it'll be at a different level. I've always looked at racing as a hobby, and riding the classic will be exactly that. I'll race it out of the back of my van and I can come first, last or do whatever I want and who gives a damn? I'm looking forward to racing without all the hype.

You already know I have had no problem finding other things to do away from the racing. My life never stops, but if it did I couldn't stand it. I'm always the same: sometimes it gets too much and I think I just want to do nothing, but I can only stand half an hour of that and I'm itching to go again.

The pushbiking opened my eyes to other kicks, the passion of riding my pushbike for long distances. I have the next race in mind: the North Cape 4000, starting in Florence in Italy, and ending in North Cape, Norway, the most northerly point of mainland Europe. And then there's Magadan, but I'm not sure when that'll be.

As I warned in the preface, the stories that make up this book were written soon after they happened, when my memory was fresh, but also without the kind of perspective that hindsight gives you. If I sounded like I was being a wanker at times, it might be because I was, but hopefully I've given enough background to everything so you can see where I was coming from, even if you don't agree with my point of view.

There's still plenty on my plate. Trying to break the Nürburgring van lap record in the Transit; building the 300mph-in-a-mile Hayabusa; competing in the North Cape 4000, maybe as early as 2018; racing the BSA; building the Nissan GTR-powered Ford pickup for Pikes Peak 2020. And we'd like to go on a family holiday to Tel Aviv or Bethlehem.

We didn't have Dot when I started this book and now she's nine months old, doing grand and always smiling. She's the greatest thing and I'd do anything for her.

Sharon's definitely the best mum, but I'm not the best dad, because I'm work and shed, work and shed, but I do the best I can. They don't want for much, except for a bit more of my time. Sharon still can't understand why I put so many hours in at the truck yard. I don't need to work as hard as I do for the money, but my life's not like that. If you have to ask why I work all the time you don't understand me. I could have all the money in the world and I'd still work my cock off. My head needs it.

When he was working, my dad was like Boxer from George Orwell's *Animal Farm*: any problem, any confrontation, can be solved by burying yourself in work, and that's rubbed off on me. I don't think it's a bad way to be.

I don't understand it myself sometimes, but I don't argue against it.

I am getting into the habit of having Saturday afternoons off because I want to spend them with Shazza and Dot. We go out to walk a goat – Shazza likes goats – or we visit a country house or park.

I like being Dad. I like that they're relying on me. It's given me a bit of responsibility outside of my own shit. I'm usually such a selfish bastard, and everything's about me building stuff, but I like this bit of compromise and the further down the line we get the more I enjoy it.

There are times I have Dot in the pram with me while I'm working in the shed, but it isn't long before Sharon comes and fetches her. She says she doesn't want Dot near any fumes, but it's not bad in my shed. Just before writing this we were in the shed with The Cult on in the background while I was working on the Transit engine.

I'm looking forward to more of that. I'm looking forward to more of everything.

INDEX

GM indicates Guy Martin.

INDEX